YUKON QUEST
SLED DOG
RACE

YUKON QUEST SLED DOG RACE

Elizabeth "Libbie" Martin

ARCADIA
PUBLISHING

Published by Arcadia Publishing
Charleston, South Carolina

Printed in the United States of America

Library of Congress Control Number: 2012943397

For all general information, please contact Arcadia Publishing:
Telephone 843-853-2070
Fax 843-853-0044
E-mail sales@arcadiapublishing.com
For customer service and orders:
Toll-Free 1-888-313-2665

Visit us on the Internet at www.arcadiapublishing.com

Dedicated to the amazing men and women who challenge
themselves and nature, pushing the limits of endurance
and comfort, and to the canine athletes that are
strong, eager, and born to run.

And to my three Muses: Corinne, Casey Jean, and Rika—
you make me soar.

CONTENTS

ACKNOWLEDGMENTS

No writer works alone; it takes many people to get a manuscript of this magnitude to completion. The author is grateful to the following for making this a possibility:

LeRoy and Katherine planted the idea into my head, loaning me the scrapbooks and giving their valuable time and memories to my digital recorder. A huge, huge, HUGE thank-you goes to Sam Harrel of the *Fairbanks Daily News-Miner* for allowing me to dig through and use numerous photographs from the paper's coverage of the race; and to Bob Eley, sportswriter at the *Fairbanks Daily News-Miner* and owner of the Fairbanks Community and Dog Mushing Museum, for all his help with photographs and answers to questions. Appreciation goes to Sara Martin, for proofing the many iterations of this manuscript and giving me valuable, if hard to hear, advice on its readability; and suggesting what would ultimately be the final format. Joan O'Leary of Forget-Me-Not Transcription Service took the hours of voice recordings and turned them into Word documents. Tank, Marti, Lori, Julie, Barbara, Frog, and Fletch, and Lance, Sebastian, Brent, Sonny, and the Daves (Dalton and Klumb) answered my incredibly dense questions and gave me a thorough and amazing education on the mushing lifestyle. Thanks also go to all the fans, board members, mushers, and other people who shared their love of this race with me. Kent Sturgis at Epicenter Press read the final manuscript and gave me his always appreciated comments and compliments. A special thank-you goes to the mushers, dogs, handlers, volunteers, fans, and supporters of the Quest for ensuring the continuation of this dream.

I conducted interviews with LeRoy and Katherine; Marti Steury, former and current executive director of the Yukon Quest, Fairbanks; Julie Estey, former executive director, Fairbanks; Sonny Lindner, musher, first winner of the Yukon Quest; John "Tank" Graham, volunteer and charter member; and mushers Dave Dalton, Dave Klumb, Lance Mackey, Brent Sass, and Sebastian Schneulle.

Kathleen Shank kept every document, newspaper clipping, and picture generated, published, taken, or otherwise produced during the early years of the Yukon Quest, putting them into three scrapbooks. I am indebted to her meticulous cataloging preservation. Without her, many of these documents would have been lost, and the history of this amazing race would be thinner and, ultimately, less satisfying.

Photographs are attributed to the organization and/or photographer, if known. Some photographs from later races have been included. Abbreviations for photograph credits are as follows: Yukon Quest Alaska (YQA), LeRoy and Kathleen Shank (Shank), *Fairbanks Daily News-Miner* (FDNM), and Elizabeth Martin (EM). If an attribution is missing, the blame is all mine.

INTRODUCTION

The day started early, before the weak rays of the February sun showed over the horizon. Temperatures hovered around minus 20 degrees Fahrenheit. In the darkness broken only by headlights, the parking lot began filling with trucks. Old, rattletrap pickups with more rust than paint slid into previously assigned spots, finding themselves next to newer, shiny behemoths. The boxes on the trucks also varied in age, size, and degree of skill used in construction. Some were old, built of scrounged, recycled wood and rusty fixtures polished to a dull sheen. Here and there, a pair of eyes stared through mesh-covered holes spaced regularly along the boxes. Occasionally, the older boxes shook slightly as the occupants turned to find a different position.

The snow in the lot was long packed down and slick, requiring care when walking. LeRoy Shank stood at the entrance to the parking lot, flanked by two men. Their faces were unseen, wrapped in scarves and hidden by fur-lined hoods. Only their breath, forming clouds around their ruffs, hinted at signs of life—unless a car or truck came creeping toward the parking lot, then the two sprang to life, walking over to the errant vehicle to tell the driver this was forbidden territory and pointing vaguely in other directions. Only when the driver could prove he or she was supposed to be there did they stand aside and wave the vehicle through.

Others, similarly clad, with huge mittens or thick gloves on their hands and sturdy cold-weather boots on their feet, milled about. Some talked with the drivers of the vehicles; others searched lists and made notes on clipboards. A few, new to the Far North, cursed useless ballpoint pens as they scratched invisible notes on paper. Ink freezes in below-zero temperatures, but no one thought to explain that to the new guys. Those who lived in this inhospitable climate used old-fashioned lead pencils to make notes. Some took pity on the "cheechakos" (tenderfeet) and handed them pencils to enable them to finish their tasks.

Everyone was ready, but no one was more ready than the 26 men and women and their 400 or so huskies in the staging area. This was the culmination of thousands of hours of training, discipline, time, and hope. It was their day.

The 26 mushers who started the first Yukon Quest were quite different. Some were professional mushers, meaning they had big kennels and sponsors, allowing them to work with their dogs full-time. Others were smaller mushers, with smaller kennels and full-time jobs besides racing. Some were trappers entering a big race for the first time. They all put in many hours preparing for the race, gathering the required gear and repairing gear that needed it.

The food drop preparation alone took most of them at least a week, as they had to gather food, divide it for drop points, bag it, divide gear into drop points, bag that. Each musher had a list for each bag; he or she had to go down that list line by line, checking everything, then checking again before sealing the burlap bag. They all marked the bags with their names and checkpoints, making sure each bag weighed no more than 60 pounds.

They had to think about what might go wrong and what they might need, because once they were on the trail, they could not acquire or replace anything unless it came from the bags sent ahead. Although family and friends were willing to help, in the end, it is the mushers who rely on each item being in the bag it is supposed to be in; they checked the bags personally to ensure everything was where it should be.

After all, when you are out on the trail with 12 very hungry dogs looking expectantly at you, you cannot tell them, "Well, there's supposed to be food here." You cannot blame someone else, because it is your responsibility to have the food or booties or a change of dry socks. Obsessive-compulsive behavior can mean the difference between life and death in the Yukon.

The 26 mushers who started the first Quest were (in starting order; with the number of dogs they started with in parentheses):

David "Pecos" Humphrey (12)
Sonny Lindner (9)
Bill Cotter (10)
Joe Runyan (12)
Jeff King (11)
Bruce Johnson (11)
Nick Ericson (10)
Mary Shields (10)
Bob English (9)
Gerald Riley (12)
Jack G. Stevens (12)
Harry Sutherland (10)
Jack Hayden (10)
Frank Turner (10)
Don Glassburn (11)
David Klumb (10)
Lorrina Mitchell (8)
Chris Whaley (12)
Ron Aldrich (12)
John Two Rivers (12)
Shirley Liss (8)
Darryle Adkins (10)
Murray Clayton (11)
Wilson Sam (12)
Senley Yuill (10)
Kevin Turnbough (11)

Race marshal Carl Huntington and race judge Leo Olesen were at the staging area, checking their lists. Head pilot Scott Spencer briefed his "Quest Air Force" pilots; they checked their planes, making sure everything was a go for the race.

Shank smiled, content. He could hardly believe the day had actually arrived—a day he dreamed about and worked for tirelessly. He barely noticed the cold temperature, the sting of the wind on his exposed skin, the tingle of excitement filling the air. This was the culmination of his big dream, the start of a race he invented and nursed through to fruition. It was his day—the Yukon Quest International Sled Dog Race, his baby—and he was thrilled.

As the sun peeked its pale face over mountains unseen through the winter haze, the final participants pulled into their parking spaces. Around them, earlier arrivals were in the throes of final preparation: dogs released from their boxes and tied to hooks welded around truck bodies; wooden sleds, large and cumbersome when awkwardly sitting in the lot, being loaded with food, sleeping bags, clothing, and dog food. Mushers busily organized their sleds, checking everything two or three times, barking (literally) orders to family members and handlers. They were focused; all they saw was what was in front of them—1,000 miles of wilderness and too many possibilities for disaster to take any chances.

It was bedlam: people yelling, dogs barking, vehicles rumbling—a cacophony that was overwhelming for most bystanders. Veteran distance-racing mushers recognized the sheer chaos that was the start of a long-distance, multiteam race. Dogs that had trained for months were so excited they howled in delight. One husky howling is music; a team is a symphony. Twenty-six teams is more music than any ear can cope with. Add to that thousands of people eager to be part of history, and the crowd's noise and exuberance and tension and anxiety and joy and fear, all rolled into one massive cloud of excitement.

This first time, many teams were not veteran racing teams, but teams used to pulling heavily loaded sleds long distances in the silence and emptiness of the bush. They were not used to crowds or confusion. When it came time to start, Glassburn's lead dog was so spooked by the pandemonium surrounding him he turned tail and ducked under his teammates on the towline, as if to say, "You can have it, I quit." Glassburn calmly pulled him out from under the other dogs and led him down the street.

Shank was not bothered by the confusion and disorder. He was enervated, knowing it would soon be quiet after the last team passed through the chute toward the first checkpoint. Musher English, No. 9, also felt no agitation. He strolled the staging area, calm, drinking a beer. It helped, he thought, that everyone else was more nervous than he was.

Johnson nervously checked his sled, borrowed from race veterinarian Carl Monetti after Johnson's sled lost a runner the day before. He did not like using a vital piece of equipment he knew nothing about, but he also was not going to sacrifice the money and time he had put into getting this far, so he did what he could to assure the sled would get him to Whitehorse relatively unscathed.

Marti Steury, executive director of the race organization, made sure everything was going smoothly. She was a recreational musher who arrived in Fairbanks courtesy of the US Army and never left. Steury had fallen into the directorship by chance, and she put hours into getting to this day. Everything was set up, teams and trucks were in place, and everything was good. No one could think or talk with that noise, a din that went beyond high decibels.

Steury walked down Second Avenue, where the race would start. She saw musher Turnbough, from Grand Marais, Minnesota, who was a minister in his day job, and she went to talk to him. She had a St. Christopher medal she wanted to give to Klumb, "the maniac who got me into mushing, who is an atheist, by the way." She wanted the medal to be blessed before giving it to him.

"Can you do me a favor?" she asked Turnbough. And though he was about to start a 1,000-mile race, with hundreds of concerns and worries and thoughts in his head, she held out the St. Christopher's medal and showed it to him. "Can you bless this and the race?"

"And in the middle of downtown Second Avenue," Steury recalled 26 years later, "with more than 400 screaming huskies, I put out my hand with the St. Christopher's medal and he put both hands over mine. And everything went dead silent. He gave the sweetest blessing, asking God to look out for all the mushers, all the dogs, and everybody out on the trail going off into the great unknown. When he got done, I took his hands away and insanity reigned again. It was one of those 'wow' moments."

Steury joined Shank in the staging area. They were joined by Roger D. Williams, the race's cofounder. They were silent; there was so much noise, they were not able to hold a decent conversation anyway. As the trucks arrived, they growled and whined as they pulled into their spots, with some of the older ones belching smoke. Chains clanked as they tied the dogs out and pulled their sleds down.

Voices—yelling, calling, talking—there were so many voices that no one could make out what anyone said. It was cold, bitterly so; they felt the sting of dry, arctic air biting their cheeks and fingers. People moved in what seemed to be chaotic randomness—officials preparing for the start; checkers looking at the sleds; handlers assisting with packing and hooking up dogs; mushers talking to every dog, praising each for its strength and beauty and life; security trying to maintain some sense of order; and fans of all ages pushing in for a closer look at their favorites, pointing cameras at the mushers, the trucks, the dogs.

Shank and Steury both smiled as they watched the mushers chain loaded sleds to pickups before harnessing the teams, knowing it was not so much for convenience as for control. The snowmachines started their growls at this point, as their drivers prepared to attach the loaded and harnessed teams to their machines. They were there to get the sled to the starting line and keep it steady and in place until the musher officially started. As the mushers drove their teams to the starting line, the snowmachine was hooked to the back, acting as a brake to hold the dogs in check until the starter said, "Go."

And now, the dogs started to sing. It started out quietly: first, a little whine, a "woo woo woo" up the scale as the dogs, sensing the excitement of the crowd and knowing they were going to run, were hooked to the truck. The dogs trembled with excitement, their tails sweeping the snow rapidly. They knew. They had known for days. And they were ready.

One dog started—it lifted that graceful wolflike muzzle into the sky and let out a howl that brought up the hairs on everyone's arms. But it was not a frightening sound; it was pure joy coming out of that throat—joy for the run, joy for the musher, joy of being alive. Soon, one of its teammates took up the song, but filling it with the same joy as the first. Another one began, then another, sometimes a bit off-key, and, finally, the entire team was howling its delight at living in this great world that let sled dogs run on the snow.

Then, the team at the next truck, hooked up waiting, joined in the chorus. And before anyone knew it, hundreds of huskies were singing their enthusiasm and excitement. The roar of the crowd, the cold, the chaos—all this was forgotten as Shank, Steury, the mushers and handlers, the volunteers, and the bystanders listened to the dogs. Theirs was an ancient tune of long-ago adventure, tales of danger and death. Underneath was the promise of gold and the lure of a journey, the quest man has always undertaken, even when the odds were long and success improbable.

1

DRIVING DOGS

Dog mushing is the official sport of Alaska. There are mushers with small yards and mushers with big ones. Some kennels are big budget, others shoestring. Some race obsessively, running any race they can; others run fewer races as dictated by time, family, full-time jobs, and finances.

People run dogs for many reasons: some want to live for the Alaska of old, the tradition of being a part of a storied history; others love a challenge, and running a team of highly intelligent huskies in Alaskan winters is most definitely a challenge; others sort of fall into it. They get one or two dogs, and, as with eating potato chips, cannot stop—pretty soon, they have 12 or 13. What else does one do with a baker's dozen of Alaskan huskies but harness them to a sled and yell "Hike!"? It is an addictive sport, and like most addictions, it is lifelong and expensive.

Native Alaskans used dogs to pull sleds and for hunting. When the first gold-seekers arrived in Alaska during the gold rush, they adopted many Native traditions, including dog sledding. With most of the goldfields in inaccessible mountains, supplies had to be barged in during the summer and hauled to camps. In the winter, the only way to get anywhere was by foot or dog sled.

Modern distance races are tests of strength, skill, and endurance in the world's harshest, most extreme environment. They cross treacherous terrain, frozen and broken ice, and go through waist-high snow, punishing winds, whiteout blizzards, and cold so deep it gets into the bones. Those who finish have good dogs, strength, iron will, and stubbornness. They do not quit, no matter how difficult it gets.

People are injured; sometimes dogs die. It's not an easy sport.

It is just the musher and the dogs out there, everything working smoothly, everyone pulling together. They do not think about the race, just the run. The dogs are their buddies. There is nothing like running a dog team in the moonlight; all around is silence, with nothing but the sounds of the snow crunching under the sled and the dogs breathing. One does not have to worry about the trail, because the dogs are doing what they are supposed to be doing; a musher does not have to watch every inch of the trail. Dogs are more dependable than snowmachines, and quieter, too.

LeRoy Shank and Roger D. Williams, fathers of the 1,000-mile race between Fairbanks, Alaska, and Whitehorse, Yukon Territory, wanted to recapture some of the rich history of the sport, the long tradition of depending on dogs for survival, and the thrill of mastering a challenging environment.

They dreamed of the Yukon Quest.

There are recreational mushers and competitive mushers, mushers with small kennels of four to eight dogs and mushers with 70 or more. Some kennels are big-budget affairs, with fancy gear and equipment and shiny custom dog trucks plastered with sponsors' names. Other mushers run kennels on shoestring budgets and drive beat-up pickups with homemade dog boxes in the beds and funky sleds strapped to the tops. (YQA; photograph by Steve Brunaski.)

A team crosses some of the vast wilderness during the race. Racing sled dogs as sport probably began around the 1850s. Some believe the first dog sled race took place as a challenge among travelers going between St. Paul, Minnesota, and Winnipeg, Canada. The St. Paul Winter Carnival featured sled dog races beginning in 1886 and still does to this day. (Shank.)

　　　　　　　　　　　　　　　　　　　　　　　　　DRIVING DOGS

Native Alaskans used dogs to haul water, fuel, and meat. They caught and dried chum salmon during the summer, feeding it to the dogs during the winter. Dogs are still vital to those who live "off the grid"—hunters, trappers, and Natives. (YQA.)

Haywood Gates's $2,000 dog team prepares to leave Dawson City in the 1899 image below. Gold miners used dog teams to get nuggets to a port city, where the gold was transferred to ships. With no roads, and rivers frozen most of the year, dog teams were the only way to get supplies in and gold out. (YQA; from Selid Collection, Alaska & Polar Regions Collections & Archives, University of Alaska Fairbanks.)

Haywood Gates' $2000 Dog Team, Dawson Y. T., 1899

WINNER FIRST PLACE.

COL. RAMSAY'S ENTRY, 3RD ALL ALASKA SWEEPSTAKES, JOHN JOHNSON, DRIVER.

The first All Alaska Sweepstakes, a race of about 400 miles held in 1909, was quite slow—about 100 hours. Most mushing dogs were freighters—they had to be big to haul heavy sleds over long distances. The record—74 hours and a few minutes—was set in 1910 with a team of all Siberian huskies owned by Fox Maule Ramsey and driven by Iron Man Johnson. That record was unbroken until 100 years later, when six finishers shattered it. (Library of Congress; photograph by Lomen Bros.)

Explorer Roald Engebreth Gravning Amundsen (1872–1928) is pictured in 1920. Amundsen used Alaskan huskies for his famous expeditions. Alaska's dogs are strong, bred to pull and endure in a harsh, inhospitable climate. Their superiority has been recognized by Arctic explorers across the world in journeys ranging from Amundsen's quest for the North Pole to Vilhjalmur Stefansson's expeditions searching for unknown lands and charting Northern waters. (Library of Congress; photograph by Lomen Bros.)

This dog team pulls a sled through a snow-covered field as two men with snowshoes walk behind them; snow-covered mountains and a placid lake are in the background. (Frank and Frances Carpenter Collection, Library of Congress, gift of Mrs. W. Chapin Huntington; 1951/public domain.)

Huskies are more stubborn than any human beings. The reality is that if they are a person's best friends, they will do everything within their living power to give that person what they want—as long as they know the person is willing to do the same. (EM.)

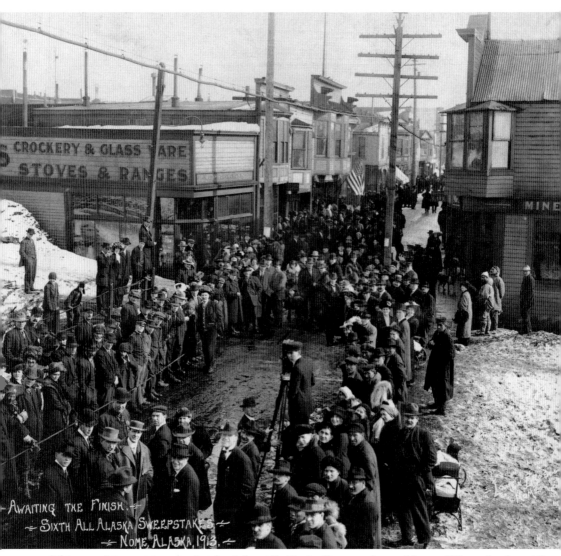

Awaiting the Finish.
Sixth All Alaska Sweepstakes
Nome, Alaska, 1913.

This crowd is awaiting the finish of the All Alaska Sweepstakes in Nome. When the first All Alaska Sweepstakes was conceived in 1909, Scotty Allan, a former horse handler, used his knowledge and experience to determine the route and made dog care a fundamental aspect of the race. The overriding sentiment—that the dogs must be tended to before the driver and that dog safety and well-being comes before even winning—still permeates the races in Alaska. (Frank and Frances Carpenter Collection, Library of Congress, gift of Mrs. W. Chapin Huntington; 1951/public domain.)

2

PRE-RACE JITTERS

Race marshal Carl Huntington and race judge Leo Olesen gathered the mushers together for a final pre-race briefing and to go over the rules one more time. Even though they had heard them the previous day and studied the rule book, the mushers listened patiently. There was no room for error in the Bush, and they knew that.

The race marshal's word is law on the trail; there is no appeal. The mushers listened to him carefully; since this was the first race, all of them were considered rookies—even veteran mushers. They had to know what they could and could not do and—most important of all—that dog care was the first and foremost priority. They were reminded the race was a test of their survival skills, meaning no outside assistance allowed except during the mandatory 36-hour layover in Dawson City. If anyone besides the musher touched the dogs or sled or assisted in any way, the musher was disqualified.

The mushers had already started the mind games and psychological deceptions that occur during a long-distance race. They looked at each other sideways, trying not to let on that they were sizing up the opponents. Lorrina Mitchell showed up at the first meeting in a very feminine dress and high heels; the men had a hard time imagining her hunkering down in minus 40 degrees Fahrenheit weather with no access to a shower or laundry facilities for two weeks. How tough could she be? "Good," she thought. "If that means the guys underestimate me, so much the better."

Watching them, LeRoy Shank thought back to the days before the race—long, grueling days making sure everything was ready. The mushers had only one job—to run the race and win it, if they could. Shank, Marti Steury, Roger D. Williams, and everyone else involved with the race organizations—one in Fairbanks, the other in Whitehorse—had to do everything else. The ultimate goal was to make sure the mushers could do their jobs.

The final 24 hours before the race were packed with 11th-hour chores, meetings, drawing numbers, and getting ready. Mushers converged on the stores in Fairbanks, filling last-minute needs or trying to replace anything they had forgotten; everyone wanted something, and they wanted it at the same time. Samson's Hardware, an early sponsor and the best place to get everything related to mushing, did what it could to meet every need.

The mushers also had to contend with the press. This race generated big buzz; there were representatives from Alaskan, Lower 48, and Canadian newspapers. The veteran mushers did not mind, but the rest of the mushers were not used to so much attention and had little to no experience with a news-hungry press—it was just one more thing to be anxious about.

A crisis occurred late in the day: Darryle Adkins smashed his sled in an accident; he did not have a spare. However, Fairbanks is the Golden Heart City with a large mushing community—numerous sled builders and mushers live in or around Alaska's second-largest city. Adkins roused John Gleason, and the two of them built a sled in record time—three and a half hours—so Adkins could make the gate on Saturday morning.

Hours before the start, crowds lined Second Avenue, the streets, the chute, and the frozen Chena River, filling every available space—more than 15,000 people came out to the inaugural Quest. It was clear and cold, around minus 20 degrees Fahrenheit. Temperatures started dropping early, falling to nearly minus 40 degrees Fahrenheit by nightfall. (YQA.)

David "Pecos" Humphrey, age 33, hailed from Talkeetna. He moved to Alaska in 1973 courtesy of the US Air Force; he started running dogs in 1976 and used a team for trapline work. During the summer, Humphrey worked for the Alaska Railroad; winter found him running a trapline on Clear Creek. (YQA; photograph by Mike Belrose.)

Sonny Lindner, age 34, was the first "name" musher to throw his sled into the ring. He worked as a general contractor in the summer and a musher during the winter, a common scenario for serious mushers. His home and kennel, Johnson River Kennel, was only accessible by dog team or airplane. (FDNM; photograph by Brian O'Donoghue.)

Bill Cotter of Nenana, age 32, began his mushing career in 1972. He was a general contractor during the summer months. He claimed to have raced in every sprint race in the state and a few mid-distance ones. His kennel was River Runners Racing Kennel; he was self-sponsored. (FDNM.)

Joe Runyan, Tanana musher and commercial fisherman, claimed no special training methods or strategies, just "the standard approach." He watched *The Adventures of Rin Tin Tin* as a kid and always swore he would own a dog when he grew up. Now, he owned 12, and they were going on that Yukon Quest together. (YQA; photograph by J. Correia.)

As they await the start, the dogs yelp and jump in excitement, their breath puffing steam clouds before their faces. The condensation soon creates frost ruffs around their eyes and mouths, but they are huskies—they laugh at cold and frost. (FDNM; photograph by Nora Gruner.)

PRE-RACE JITTERS

Race officials have deputies because the mushers do not arrive and leave at the same time. Since the race prides itself on offering the same care for the Red Lantern winner (the last finisher) as the first-place team, there have to be officials at all checkpoints until the last musher has passed through. Generally, the head officials follow the front-runners because that part of the race is where the most issues arise; deputies handle the rest. (EM.)

The race starts in Fairbanks on even years; mushers stage in the Fairbanks North Star Borough Building parking lot and maneuver down to the starting line on the Chena River. It takes numerous volunteers—and often a snowmachine—to keep the dogs from jumping the start. In the first race, founders set a maximum limit of 12 dogs per team, allowing only three dropped dogs so mushers started with a better team, took better care of that team, and ran a slower, more thoughtful race. There was not the option of taking marginal, or "spare," dogs. The rule fit into the philosophy of a small, simple, low-cost race accessible to mushers big and small. (FDNM.)

Jeff King was a general contractor from Denali Park. He started mushing in 1977 by buying some dogs, building a cabin, and running a trapline on the Nenana River. He also ran Denali Dog Tours and Wilderness Freighters; his Husky Enterprise Kennels gave him the 12 dogs that took him to Whitehorse. (YQA.)

Bruce Johnson, age 37, of Atlin, British Columbia, was the first Canadian to put his money into the hat. Johnson was a veteran distance musher and quite at home in the terrain because of his occupation as a wilderness outfitter. He ran his dogs under the name Johnson Sled Dogs. (YQA.)

Nick Ericson, age 21, of Fairbanks, was the youngest entrant in 1984. He worked as a carpenter to afford his small team. The Quest was his first race, and he said he was running "for the scenery and T-shirt." Ericson had no handler and was self-sponsored. He did his training around the Interior. (FDNM.)

Mary Shields, a longtime musher from Schimmelpfennig Creek, was a 16-year musher at the time of the race. She moved to Alaska from Wisconsin in 1965. In this photograph, she booties a dog after putting ointment on a cut. (FDNM; photograph by Mike Mathers.)

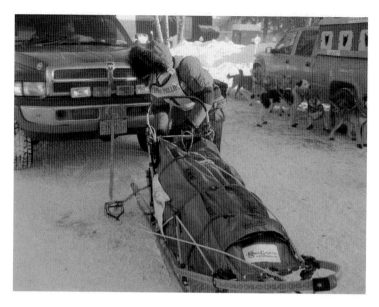

Long-distance sleds are large and designed to carry the heavy loads required over long distances between checkpoints. As they pack, mushers check their sleds, sometimes two or three times, to make sure they have the required equipment, food, and other gear; failure to include certain things could result in penalties or disqualification. (EM.)

A team waits in the truck boxes to be harnessed. As each truck pulls into its assigned spot, the dogs in the boxes stir restlessly. Some howl or bark to voice their enthusiasm; others whine eagerly, knowing they will soon fulfill their destiny. A few lift their noses, sniffing noisily and taking in the exhilarating odors that waft through the bitterly cold air. (FDNM.)

PRE-RACE JITTERS

Alaskan huskies can lope more than 20 miles per hour for up to 30 miles. In distance races, most teams go 10 to 15 miles per hour for up to 150 miles a day. With the right mix of running and rest, a top team of 12 dogs and a musher can run the 1,000 miles of the Quest in 10 days, running up to 12 hours a day in the worst conditions imaginable. (FDNM.)

For 10 years, Bob English, a 41-year-old city employee from Whitehorse, had been racing in sprint and distance races with dogs out of his Crowley Kennels. He said of himself: "My special talents include drinking scotch and, if nothing else, rum. I have received no honors but am notorious." (FDNM; photograph by Eric Muehling.)

Jack Stevens of Sunshine, age 34, was an equipment operator who ran and won several open championships and other long-distance races. Growing up in Canada and Colorado, Stevens called himself a dog person for life. He provided dog trips and ran traplines in the Talkeetna Mountains. (FDNM.)

Harry Sutherland, age 43, of Delta Junction, ran dogs for about 12 years while working on a trapline. He was a carpenter in the off season (summer) and built his own home, which was only accessible by dog sled, on Dry Creek. He personally financed his run. (FDNM.)

In this photograph, an unidentified team leaves Fairbanks at the start of the Yukon Quest. Psychologically, the first spot out of the gate is the worst; no musher wants to be first to start. In any race, it means his dogs will be breaking trail for those behind. In 1984, it meant being the guinea pig for an untried route and unknown checkpoints. By "luck" of the draw, Dave "Pecos" Humphrey made history as the first musher to leave the gate for the inaugural Yukon Quest. He joked: "Maybe I'll be a trivia question 10 years from now." (YQA.)

Self-contained and self-dependent, a team races through the lonely landscape. LeRoy Shank approached veteran dog musher and Antarctic explorer Col. Norman D. Vaughan to be the keynote speaker for the first Draw Banquet on February 23; Vaughn epitomized the spirit of the North. "Mushing is one of the great things about Alaska," Vaughn told the audience. "And this will become one of its greatest events. It's the only international sled dog race of its kind, and it will get larger next year." This was the night before the big day—the culmination of many dreams and months of hard work—and few could believe the race they had dreamed about and spent so many hours organizing, cajoling, massaging, and babying was finally only hours away. More than 300 people attended the banquet—mushers, handlers, officials, volunteers, and fans. (FDNM.)

　　　　　　　　　　　　　　　　　　　　　　　PRE-RACE JITTERS

3

...AND THEY'RE OFF

Yukon Quest volunteer attorney Joe Paskvan stood at the starting area, watching the culmination of months of work. "It was high intensity," he recalled years later. "Everyone is just believing [he or she is] part of something bigger than just Fairbanks or just a musher. It was just truly something."

While Paskvan has never been a musher, he admires the toughness of the competitors and their willingness to face the wilderness and harsh challenges, just to say they did. For a moment, the young man thought maybe he would try it one day, before age and life got to him, just to say he had done it.

The race began promptly at 11:00 a.m. Mushers left every two minutes. The dogs shot out of the gate, looking like sprinters heading for a record. Trying to slow these dogs down was almost impossible.

Not all the starts were letter-perfect. Bruce Johnson, on his borrowed sled, saw his dogs take a sightseeing detour to the left down Noble Street instead of heading right and toward the river. Two of Senley Yuill's dogs got tangled up in their lines. He stopped the sled, ran forward, untangled his dogs, and watched his sled soar past. The crowd roared in delight as Yuill took a flying leap onto his runners. The dogs did not miss a beat.

When Kevin Turnbough's team left the chute, Marti Steury breathed a sigh of relief. The start was over, and no disasters had occurred. LeRoy Shank, acting as race director, rushed out to checkpoint no. 1 at Chena Hot Springs. His job was just beginning, but as he drove, he could not help thinking back on how he got to this day.

The Yukon Quest International Sled Dog Race was born on August 27, 1980, when Shank, his wife, Kathleen, Roger D. Williams, Willy Lipps, and Ron Rosser got an idea for a different kind of competition after running a 125-mile race on Angel Creek.

While winding down at the Bull's Eye Saloon, they tossed out ideas for a new long-distance race. Basically, as they imagined it, it would be an expansion of the Bull's Eye–Angel Creek 125 race and cover a distance of 1,000 miles.

"I don't like to have people think it was a barroom thing," Williams told a reporter after the first race. "That was the fun part, and then the work started."

Shank was interested in a race that challenged the team, highlighting the athleticism of the dogs and the self-sufficiency of the musher. He also wanted a race that belonged to Fairbanks. Williams was interested in the historical aspect—the gold rush and mail-delivery routes from the start of the 20th century that passed by the roadhouses (or their derelict remains) that kept travelers warm and safe in the days before airplanes, automobiles, and other reliable transportation.

They brainstormed a route. There was a lot of laughing and tons of ideas, but in no way did any of the friends think the Yukon Quest International Sled Dog Race would ever happen. As usually transpires when great ideas are discussed over beer, most of them forgot about it. But not Shank. Not Williams. It stayed in their heads.

Race fans, undeterred by sub-zero temperatures, cheer from the bridge over the Chena River as Bill Cotter passes through Fort Wainwright. So many people had traveled the trails; many never left. Stampeders traveled from Fortymile and Circle, across the Yukon to the Klondike and back in search of wealth and adventure. They broke trail, going where no white man had gone before, and found vast swaths of untouched land and, sometimes, fortune. And then, just like that, the

Jack Hayden, of Lake Minchumina, arrived in Alaska in 1970. The 35-year-old trapper/contractor's Alaska jobs included gold miner, air taxi pilot, trapper, and construction worker. The Yukon Quest was his first race, but trapping, training, and hauling logs gave him plenty of time and experience with his team. (FDNM.)

. . . AND THEY'RE OFF

gold was gone; the towns and camps emptied. The river flowed past crumbling cabins, abandoned placer mines, empty tattered tents. Brush reclaimed the land as the gold rush faded into history. Now, the area is just wilderness—unpopulated, unknown. The ghosts are left alone, wandering aimlessly with no one to remember or console them. (FDNM; photograph by X. Belinsky.)

Frank Turner, a 36-year-old musher from Whitehorse, always dreamed of running a long-distance race—the Quest was his answer to that dream. He ran dogs for nine years before putting his sled to the Quest. His dogs came from his Muktuk Kennels in Whitehorse. (FDNM.)

Don Glassburn, a 35-year-old trapper/miner from Central, entered the race because his trapline ran along the route, and watching everyone having fun would be too much for him. He got most of his support from friends and neighbors who donated money and held several fundraising events for him. (YQA.)

Dave Klumb, age 28, started running dogs in 1974 and liked it so much he made it his full-time job. He called his kennel Laughing Husky Kennel because his dogs were "recruited" from the animal shelter; they were on death row until they were added to Klumb's team. That kind of tale deserves a laugh, he said. His goal was to get to Whitehorse with him, his dogs, and his sled in one piece. (FDNM.)

. . . AND THEY'RE OFF

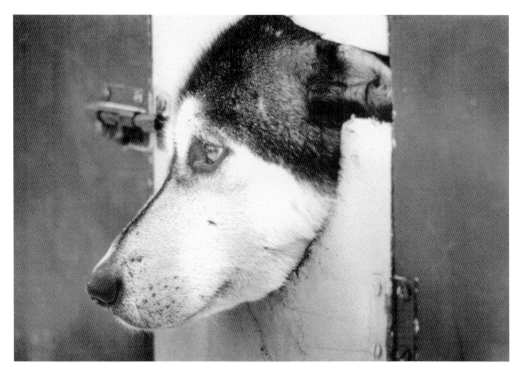

Huskies are not aggressive toward other dogs or people, as they come into contact with both constantly. Although teams will sometimes fight among themselves, they usually are even-tempered and play well with others. Alaskan huskies are gentle, playful, willful, mischievous, sociable, easygoing, and loving. (FDNM; photograph by Mike Belrose.)

Food drop coordinator Ray Mackler is buried under a mountain of supplies for the 1985 race. Mushers are responsible for planning, obtaining, and packing all the food and supplies they will need for themselves and their dogs. They divide the supplies by checkpoint, pack them in burlap bags, and take them to a central spot for delivery to the various checkpoints. (YQA.)

The Yukon Quest International Sled Dog Race was born when LeRoy Shank (left) and Roger D. Williams, along with Shank's wife, Kathleen, and some friends, got the idea for a different kind of race after running the Bull's Eye–Angel Creek 125, a 125-mile race between Bull's Eye Saloon and Angel Creek Lodge. After tossing the idea around for about three weeks, Shank decided to talk to someone in Whitehorse to see if the race were possible. He called the chamber of commerce and was eventually connected with Lorrina Mitchell, who became a Yukon-area board member. She was good friends with Wendy Waters, who also joined the original Yukon board. Waters and Mitchell took care of the Whitehorse/Canada end, and a race was born. (YQA.)

YUKON QUEST
SLED DOG RACE
1,000 MILES over the GOLD RUSH TRAIL

FAIRBANKS TO WHITEHORSE
FEBRUARY 25, 1984

$15,000 IN GOLD — FIRST PLACE

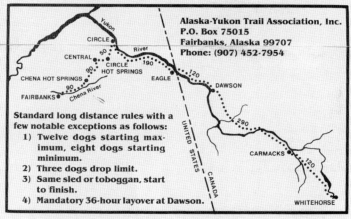

Alaska-Yukon Trail Association, Inc.
P.O. Box 75015
Fairbanks, Alaska 99707
Phone: (907) 452-7954

Standard long distance rules with a few notable exceptions as follows:
1) **Twelve dogs starting maximum, eight dogs starting minimum.**
2) **Three dogs drop limit.**
3) **Same sled or toboggan, start to finish.**
4) **Mandatory 36-hour layover at Dawson.**

The purposes for which this corporation was organized are:

1. To support long distance sled dog racing and in particular to support a sled dog race of international character between Fairbanks, Alaska and Whitehorse, Yukon Territory.

2. To provide an opportunity for and encourage participation in an epic by musher and dog, without regard to the musher's sex, race, religion, national origin, background, age, vocation or economic standing.

3. To recognize and promote the spirit that compels one to live in the Great North Land, an international spirit that knows no governmental boundaries, to bring public attention to the historic role of the Arctic Trail in the development of the North Country, and the people and animals that strove to meet its challenge.

4. To commemorate the historic dependence of man on his sled dogs for mutual survival in the Arctic Environment and to perpetuate mankind's concern for his canine companion's continued health, welfare and development.

5. To encourage and facilitate knowledge and application of the widest variety of bush skills and practices that form the foundation of Arctic Survival.

6. To offer an experience that reflects the spirit and perseverance of the pioneers who discovered themselves in their wild search for adventure, glory, and wealth in the Frozen North.

To get sponsors and mushers, LeRoy Shank put these flyers all over Fairbanks and North Pole and sent them to anyone he thought might support a Fairbanks-based long-distance race, a different kind of event in which skill and know-how mattered more than money and sponsorships. It would feature the musher and the dogs on their own, with only their wits, survival skills, and gear between them and disaster, like it was 100 years ago. After a few spots on a local radio show and columns by *Fairbanks Daily News-Miner* sports writer Bob Eley, interest was sparked. (Shank.)

There are separate boards for Alaska and Whitehorse. The formal incorporation ceremony for Sourdough Trail International, the organization that runs the business of the race, was held on October 19, 1983. The Alaska and Canada board members pictured here are, from left to right, (first row) Bud Smythe, Lorinna Mitchell, Gordon Mitchell, and Roger D. Williams; (second row) LeRoy Shank, Rod Perry, and Wendy Waters. (Shank.)

The first Yukon Quest charter members pictured here are, from left to right, Jerry Martin, Dave Klumb, Roger D. Williams, LeRoy Shank, and Jim Bennet; first executive director Marti Steury is in front. The core group of fans, mushers, and volunteers became charter members because most of the people involved not only worked for free—they contributed money as well. (FDNM; photograph by Jocelyn S. Williams.)

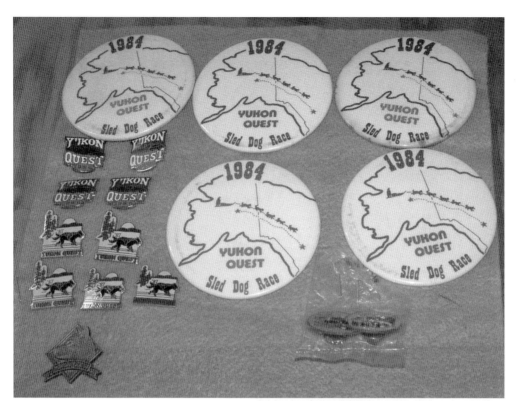

LeRoy Shank knew marketing was a key to getting money, sponsors, and fans, so he made sure there were pins and buttons for sale. A local artist is contracted to design a new, unique pin and patch every year; realistically, in terms of marketing, one has to assume no one has heard of the race and make each year as memorable as the first year. (EM.)

This image shows the first Yukon Quest office in Fairbanks. It was a shoestring operation, this first Quest—even before the name was chosen, the organizers started to chase funding, most of which came in small chunks. (FDNM; photograph by Mike Mathers.)

In the days before GPS, organizers pored over maps to align their vision and history with reality and feasibility. They found volunteers in Alaska and Canada to break trails and mark them with more than 5,000 lathe stakes, making sure each section matched with the sections on either side. (YQA.)

Fewer checkpoints and more mandatory gear was a nod to the distance between checkpoints. Siwashing on the trail required winter camping knowledge and the right kind of equipment in the correct amounts. No one wanted to see anyone injured, lost, or killed because of lack of planning or gear. (YQA.)

In the North, snow covers much of the ground for most of the year. Sleds with runners for gliding over snow and ice are best to get people, mail, medicine, and other necessities over the thousands of miles between communities. Dogs are easier to care for than horses: they sleep anywhere, their coats keep them warm, and they can eat moose or small animals or hunt for their own food. (YQA.)

Long-distance racing has several general rules: mushers are self-sufficient, carrying everything they will need while covering hundreds of miles across frozen wilderness with civilization and residents few and far between; they can help each other, but "pre-planned" assistance is not allowed; and animals must be treated humanely. (YQA.)

LeRoy Shank believed people who donated that first year donated to more than a sled dog race. Something else drew them in. Was it the history? Partly. But Shank thought it was the whole package—the history, dog care, and return to a focus on skill and strength over money and slick advertising. (EM.)

Early racing harnesses were trapline tandems with leather, horse-collar harnesses. After the gold rush, returning prospectors brought a gangline hitch with dogs working in pairs, using lightweight webbing harnesses. Modern harnesses are usually lightweight but strong nylon with sheepskin padding to avoid injuries caused by a rubbing harness. (YQA; photograph by Jocelyn S. Williams.)

9191—Bound for the Klondike Gold Fields, Chilcoot Pass, Alaska.

This 1898 image is captioned "Bound for Klondike Gold Fields, Chilcoot [sic] Pass, Alaska." When George Carmack discovered Bonanza Creek in 1896, the Klondike gold rush began. Miners went over the Chilcoot Pass by foot. Population estimates at the peak of the rush range from 40,000 to 50,000. More than $100 million in gold was mined, but by 1906, the easily worked placer mines were played out, and the territory emptied. As mushers in the Yukon Quest race over the ground that held Klondike stampeders in their quests for riches, the history is still a viable, tangible essence. It seeps from the ground and permeates the air, almost creating an odor of history and time. (Copyright by B.L. Singley [Keystone View Co.], No. 9191.)

The Yukon River led thousands of gold-seekers to its shores, all questing for something—be it treasure, freedom, or adventure. From the shore, men broke paths to the goldfields, building towns and camps on the way. The trails were not roads, just breaks in the thick forests, slightly packed paths through deep snow. Eventually, these were packed down into more or less permanent routes as men, sleds, horses, and dogs took the literal path of least resistance on their journeys. As civilization followed, the trails were used for ferrying supplies and mail to the camps, which grew into towns. (Library of Congress.)

. . . AND THEY'RE OFF

4

ON THE TRAIL

Early Alaskan roads were primitive trails barely visible in the lush undergrowth. Winter travel was difficult. Alaska is a very large place, and getting from one end to the other has never been easy. Trips could take weeks, so travelers stopped at roadhouses along the way to rest, get some hot food or drink, change horses or dogs, and sleep away the weariness.

The Yukon Quest trail, in addition to being a conglomeration and combination of old mining and mail trails, is rigorous. The route crosses four mountain ranges, and temperatures routinely drop to as low as minus 61 degrees Fahrenheit. Winds can reach 50 miles per hour.

The first race started on Second Avenue in Fairbanks, hitting the ice of the Chena River northeast toward checkpoint no. 1. About 17 miles out of town, the trail picked up an old sled pathway and crossed the Little Chena River, running alongside the Chena River. The first stretch ended at Chena Hot Springs.

The mushers then backtracked to the Boulder Creek Trail. Running alongside the north fork of the Chena, the trail went over the Frying Pan Creek Trail to 101 Mile Steese Highway. It then rose from 1,550 feet above sea level, 2,250 feet almost straight up Rosebud Summit (elevation 3,640 feet), down a few feet, then up again to Eagle Summit (3,685 feet). From Eagle Summit, it was a straight shot to checkpoint no. 2 at Arctic Circle Hot Springs. Then, it crossed Crooked Creek, went through Central, then on to Circle City and checkpoint no. 3.

Mushers hit the Yukon River and headed to Eagle—checkpoint no. 4. From here, the distance between checkpoints stretched into lonely miles of ice and cold.

From Eagle, the trail ran up the Yukon and Klondike Rivers, up Bonanza and El Dorado Creeks, and over the Black Hills to the Stewart River. The trail crossed the Pelly River, the route the Northwest Mounties took as they patrolled by dog sled.

The final stretch of the first half traced the route of the old Dawson stagecoach trail into Dawson City, checkpoint no. 5. After leaving Dawson, the mushers crossed to Bonanza Creek, the epicenter of the Klondike gold rush. The trail threaded through an area of mining waste following the Klondike River. The mushers then summited King Solomon's Dome—easily the highest point of the race at an elevation of 4,002 feet. They hit checkpoint no. 6 at Carmacks, the last official checkpoint before the finish line in Whitehorse, in front of the White Pass & Yukon Route Railroad Depot.

Once the general route was set, the hard work began. The group met every night for months, often late into the night. Shank began talking up his idea everywhere he could.

Bob Eley, sportswriter for the *Fairbanks Daily News-Miner*, kept the ink flowing. In a column written on the occasion of the 25th anniversary of the race, Eley writes: "I can vividly remember when I was approached by a couple of co-workers [sic]—Shank and Williams—wondering what I thought about the possibility of holding a dog race that went from Fairbanks to Whitehorse. My immediate reaction was 'You're crazy,' with a few expletives in between the 'you're' and 'crazy.'" Eley admitted that perhaps he had been wrong, and his colleagues were not insane.

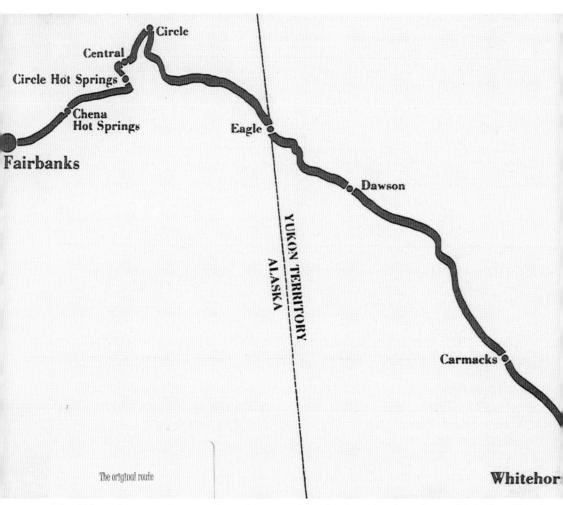

The original route

Whitehor

The Yukon Quest trail passes through some of the harshest land in the world. LeRoy Shank told the *Fairbanks Daily News-Miner* the trail was chosen because of its historical significance: "During the Gold Rush, it used to be the only way to get between [Fairbanks and Whitehorse]." Evidence of historical use of the area—trapper's cabins and fish and game wardens' cabins—was discovered as Shank and his team cleared the brush. Many trees carried old scars—blazes cut into the bark to mark the trails. The volunteers felt the history surround them as they brought the past to light. "We reconnected back to the history," Marti Steury said. "To the Old Mail Trail, to the way the freight and the mail and the food and supplies got to everywhere in the winter. This became just this huge adventure that reawakened the old history." (Shank.)

Gold was discovered on the Fortymile River in September 1886, sparking the first Interior Alaskan gold rush. Gold claims—and settlements—sprang up as thousands of miners worked the sands and gravels. In 1887, some 115 miners were using hand picks and shovels shoulder to shoulder along the sand bar at the confluence of the Fortymile and Yukon Rivers. They mined more than 14,000 ounces of gold that first year. (YQA.)

An Air Force O-2A Forward Air Control aircraft works a spotting mission south of Fairbanks during the 1986 Quest. This twin-engine light aircraft operated out of Eielson Air Force Base and provided aerial reconnaissance of the mushers during the race. (US Air Force/YQA.)

With so much space between checkpoints, mushers not only had to carry everything they might need, they had to pace themselves. The Yukon Quest re-created the environment of old, with mushers spending nights on the trail, being away from civilization longer, and relying only on themselves and their dogs for survival and success. (YQA; photograph by Stephanie Harlen.)

Mushers develop deep bonds with their dogs; they learn to read each other. The dogs are eager to please, but if the driver is only half in the race, the dog will follow the driver's lead. Mushers have to stay on their toes, because the dogs are very smart, adaptable animals. (YQA.)

ON THE TRAIL

Driver Harry Taylor coaxes his car over Thompson Pass in July 1931. As soon as cars were more reliable and roads more passable, dog teams were replaced by automobiles for the transportation of freight and passengers in Alaska. (YQA.)

The Yukon Quest board gave schoolchildren the chance to design a logo. The logo ended up coming from a Canadian student, Simon Mohamad, of Haines Junction, Yukon Territory. The 13-year-old's design was chosen from more than 70 entries from schoolchildren across Alaska and Canada. (Shank.)

The Yukon Quest logo, combining the flags of Alaska and the Yukon Territory, was designed by 13 year-old Simon Mohamad of Haines Junction, Y.T. His design was selected from nearly 70 entries from schoolchildren in Alaska and the Yukon.

The Quest trail has to be cleared each year because it is only in use during the race. It does not connect anything except traplines and recreational areas. Yet even after clearing and marking it, there are no guarantees. The weather here is excitable and always changing—the trail is never the same from day to day. (Shank.)

Fairbanks Daily News-Miner sportswriter and LeRoy Shank's colleague Bob Eley kept the race on everyone's minds with his columns. His first story took two weeks to put together—and fate hit hard when the *News-Miner*'s computers crashed just before the deadline, sending the entire story into computer limbo. Eley then put together another story in a few hours, using his prodigious memory and considerable journalistic skill, and the news went out. (FDNM; photograph by Roger D. Williams.)

Some parts of the race go through land owned by the US government. The Bureau of Land Management requires certification that all straw provided to the mushers before and through BLM lands is certified weed-free. At the end of the race, someone has to go back and make sure all the booties are cleaned up, no messes are left behind, and the straw is spread out in a proper manner so as not to leave a trace. (YQA.)

The expectations for mushers are summed up in the *Yukon Quest Rule Book*'s Rule 36, Sportsmanship: "The Code of the North dictates that all travelers be courteous, helpful, generous and honorable to a degree that will inspire and ensure enduring concern for their welfare in the minds of their hosts. Conduct yourself well enough so that the next musher will be welcomed with equal hospitality. Any competitor or athlete worthy of that name realizes that all people—officials, volunteers, media, and fans—are equally participants in this event and that it is the musher's responsibility to define the upper limits of human performance. A true Sportsman is an inspiration to all witnesses." The Spirit of the North dictates that everyone is in this together—Alaskans, Canadians, mushers, non-mushers, volunteers, and paid staffers. That means a participant helps out a fellow musher even if it means losing a lead. (FDNM.)

ON THE TRAIL

Harry Sutherland arrives at the Chena Hot Springs checkpoint, one of the first of the mushers to arrive Saturday afternoon. On the Chena River out of Fairbanks, the flat, smooth trail gradually morphs from an urban landscape to gentle rolling hills and flat meadows. The riverbank was packed with cheering fans and race supporters; people lined up to get a glimpse of this historic race. With good conditions, the 90 miles from the start of the race to checkpoint no. 1 can be covered quickly. A US Geological Survey (USGS) field surveyor discovered Chena Hot Springs in 1907. Studies have shown that the water in the hot springs has different mineral qualities than those of any other North American hot springs. In 1984, the USGS reported the springs had a daily flow of 200,000 gallons at an average temperature of 156 degrees Fahrenheit. (FDNM.)

Lorrina Mitchell, of Whitehorse, Yukon Territory, started racing when she was 16. In 1984, she was a hardy veteran of mid-distance and sprint races in the United States and Canada. Her husband, Gord, acted as her handler; her dogs came from their Pineland Kennels. (FDNM; photograph by Mike Mathers.)

Chris Whaley, a 26-year-old from College, came to Fairbanks from France in 1978; he caught the mushing bug the next year. This waiter and pastry chef was an adventurous sort, having walked the length of Oregon and Washington and bicycling to Anchorage from San Francisco. (FDNM.)

John Two Rivers, age 40, from North Pole, used his dog team for transport throughout the Interior. He worked as a general contractor, trapper, and hunter. He also bred and raised dogs. Two Rivers prepared for this race by training in terrain similar to that of the race. (FDNM.)

Trapper Creek musher Darryle Adkins, age 34, came to Alaska as a child in 1960; his family homesteaded, using dogs for transportation to the nearest road. Adkins was a full-time dog musher; he started D&E Kennels in 1981 with one dog, and by 1984, he had more than 20 good running dogs. (FDNM.)

John Two Rivers stops at Chena Hot Springs. Overnight lows at the hot springs, about 90 miles from Fairbanks, dipped to minus 20 degrees Fahrenheit on Saturday night. The next morning, two of Two Rivers' dogs were injured after crashing into a tree, then his lead dogs got tangled in a bush and were injured when the team overran them. He tried to continue, but the leaderless team faltered. Two Rivers realized this race was not going to be the cakewalk he assumed. "I thought the hard work was over," he said, thoughtfully. "Now I'm not so sure." (FDNM.)

Bob English, followed closely by Lorrina Mitchell, arrives at Chena Hot Springs checkpoint on Sunday, February 26, 1984. English missed a turn due to the myriad recreational trails along the way. Even though it was a relatively short distance, some mushers spent Saturday night on the trail. The start of a race is always hard on a team, with the excitement, stress of preparing, and the initial frenzy of the race. Resting the dogs early was a way of calming them and ensuring they would not crash and burn at the beginning of the race. (FDNM; photograph by Eric Muehling.)

ON THE TRAIL

The dogs trust the musher to keep them safe; the musher trusts the dogs to keep him safe. A musher knows how much he or she depends on the dogs as a lifeline, while the dogs are focused on pleasing the musher and running as fast as they physically can. A musher who rests his dogs when they need it—almost reading their minds—will have more success in races. The trail is in a subarctic zone: it is cold, windy, and snowy. Frostbite and hypothermia are always lurking in the background, waiting to strike. Mushers who are not prepared can suffer permanent damage from frostbite; it is not uncommon to meet mushers missing tips of toes and fingers. A musher who is injured in these extreme conditions has a serious chance of dying if he or she is not found. As the intrepid mushers arrived at each checkpoint, they stopped to let the checkers know they had arrived. Checkers made note of the time each team arrived and left, then the mandatory gear was examined. The checkers would confirm the mushers had sufficient dog food for the next stretch of trail—if they did not, they could be disqualified. (FDNM.)

Wilson Sam, of Huslia, had more than 30 years of experience with dogs; a Koyukuk native, he grew up with dogs, mushing around the Huslia area and hunting and fishing. He made his living as a trapper and fisherman and trained about 60 miles per day to prepare for the race. (FDNM.)

Kevin Turnbough, from Grand Marais, Minnesota, was a 29-year-old minister and the only "Outsider" (i.e., not Alaskan or Canadian but from "Outside") to enter the race. He entered the Quest because he saw a "certain appeal" in the challenge of testing survival and mushing skills in a race with only six checkpoints. (FDNM.)

Race veterinarian Karin Schmidt examines one of Frank Turner's dogs at the 1984 pre-race vet check. Veterinarians check every animal that will be racing. Each musher has a book for the team, and every dog gets its own page; at each checkpoint, the veterinarian makes note of the dog's condition. The record travels with the dog throughout the race—it is one of the mandatory items checked at each stop. If a veterinarian thinks a dog is in danger, he or she can force a musher to drop it; the veterinarians' decisions on dog care are final. (YQA; photograph by Mike Belrose.)

James "Tank" Graham (left), a charter member, and Loy Mac Iver, a volunteer from Portland, chip ice off the sidewalk in front of the first Yukon Quest office, at Second Avenue and Cushman Street in Fairbanks. Since the race only has a few paid staff members, volunteers run the race and office; even the board is a volunteer board. (FDNM; photograph by Rob Stapleton.)

Once at a checkpoint, the mushers picket the dogs, take off booties, check feet, medicate feet if necessary, feed the dogs, and replenish supplies from food drop bags. Sometimes, the musher will partake of hot coffee and food offered by the checkpoint volunteers. Then, if there is time, the musher can take a short nap. Checkpoints are manned 24 hours a day, seven days a week, until all mushers are accounted for (either passed through or scratched). (FDNM; photograph by X. Belinsky.)

Mushers draw their race numbers at the start banquet. Then, the dogs get metal tags with the year and their musher's number stamped on them. Volunteers manufacture the stamped tags by hand each year. (EM.)

5

WHAT'S IN A NAME?

With the Quest in full throttle, LeRoy Shank mused over the past. Now, the words "Yukon Quest" naturally rolled off people's tongues, but Shank remembered when his little dream had no name.

When Shank and his collaborators got the idea for a different kind of race, Shank knew they needed to brand the event. That required a good name, one that resonated in the minds of both mushers and non-mushers—a name that conjured up adventure and excitement. As the group worked on planning and organizing the first race, the word they needed eluded them.

Shank wanted to have final say on the name, and he wanted the name Yukon incorporated into it to mesh history with excitement; he was willing to bend on almost anything else, but not that.

"I like the name Yukon, not Yukon River. I mean the whole, a romantic name," he said. It did not much matter if it was the first or second part, because either way, the name would tell people what the race is all about.

Some of the suggestions made were accurate, but Shank did not feel a spark, and the details of organizing a new race were such that the seemingly minor issue got put on the back burner. "Nothing hit me, so we kept putting it off," Shank said. "We had T-shirts that said the 'First Annual Fairbanks to Whitehorse Sled Dog Race' ... [but] there was no name."

Someone suggested the "Thousand Mile Gold Rush," because the first racer into Dawson City gets a poke of gold. After listening to similar ideas, Kathleen Shank brought out a dictionary, and they started flipping through it. It took a while, but suddenly, something jumped out, and Kathleen blurted, "Quest." LeRoy knew immediately that it was the word he had been looking for. Kathleen read through the definition: "It says '1a: a search or hunt.'

"But I looked further, and it says under two, 'an expedition of knights,'" said Shank. "That's it. Eureka!" The Yukon Quest symbolized the search for adventure, the call of the wild, the gold rush days—it was exactly the name Shank wanted. "Before the end of the year," he said, "everybody will know what we're talking about. It's nice and short and it's easy to write, and the definition exactly captures the spirit of the race."

Starting a new race was challenging, plus bringing in the Canadians—there were times when everyone thought Shank and his team were crazy to try it. But that crossing of international boundaries underlined the whole purpose of the race—to celebrate the spirit and people of the North. Country boundaries are political; the North is more a way of life, a way of looking at the world that supersedes geopolitics and man-made dividing lines. After the first few weeks, crossing the border was no longer an issue. The biggest question was whether the teams could go 300 miles between checkpoints.

In a unique twist on international relations, the United States and Canada decided to alternate starts—in even years, the race begins in Fairbanks; in odd years, it starts in Whitehorse. This way, both cities experience the benefits and downsides of a major race.

QUEST

An expedition of Knights; there sat Arthur on the dais-thron, and those that had gone out **upon the quest,** wasted and worn . . . stood before the King.

(Tennyson)

LeRoy Shank insisted that the name Yukon be part of the race name because it invokes iconic images of adventure, romance, hardship, survival, and strength. After searching for months, his wife, Kathleen, found the perfect word, and the race became the Yukon Quest. (Shank.)

Mushing is . . . All around is wilderness. The sled runners schuss on the snow as the dogs tuck their heads down, tired from running but not willing to slow down or stop. It is cold, with sled thermometers registering temperatures of minus 30 degrees Fahrenheit. It is cold and quiet. A human could feel lost inside this big landscape, but the mushers do not. There is no place they would rather be, and no one they would rather share it with than the 12 hounds running in front of them. The mushers think about the trail to come and smile softly; this is as good as it gets. (FDNM.)

WHAT'S IN A NAME?

Huskies have a dense double coat suitable for harsh winter climates. They shed their undercoats in the spring, losing tufts of hair for three to six weeks as the weather begins to warm up. They start growing their winter coats in September or October, when the weather turns cooler. (FDNM; photograph by Mike Mathers.)

Mushers recruit one or two people to act as handlers during the race. Handlers follow the race, picking up dropped dogs or assisting the mushers as they are able. Handlers take a rest any way or place they can while waiting for the teams. (FDNM; photograph by Charles Mason.)

A picket is strung between two solid objects, usually trees, and the dogs are attached while they wait to be harnessed. Mushers rarely take dogs straight from the box or truck to the harness. The picket offers a good way to rest and feed a team while on the trail. Pickets are usually made of chain or aircraft cable with heavy-duty quick links at the ends for wrapping around trees. Individual drop lines on the pickets are light passing-link chain (not twisted) and are usually about 18 inches long. Dogs are spaced so they have room to move, but not so close that they tangle with each other. (FDNM; photograph by V. DeWitt.)

WHAT'S IN A NAME?

Crossing an international border creates all kinds of logistical challenges. When the mushers arrived in Dawson City, they had to be cleared through US Customs. In this photograph, Royal Canadian Mounted Police (RCMP) constable Andre Hoisan (left) and Dawson City manager Peter Dunbar (right) check with Wilson Sam's handler about the passports and dog records for Sam's team. (FDNM; photograph by J. Correia.)

There are some medications, especially those carried by the veterinary team, that are not supposed to pass over international borders, so clearances were needed. The dogs had to be quarantined until their handlers/mushers passed through customs and officials certified they had all been properly vaccinated. The highest standards of dog care were expected of all mushers, professional and nonprofessional alike. The Yukon Quest board recruited eight veterinarians for the first race, but no doctors or EMTs for the mushers; if something happened to humans, they had to hope the veterinarians could patch them up. (FDNM.)

Media began arriving several days before the start of the race. Most sent in their accreditation requests early, but there are always last-minute accommodations. The news media want access to the mushers, who are trying to get their heads into the race and do not want to be bothered. At every checkpoint, eager reporters converged on the frontrunners to get the scoop. (YQA.)

Handlers, if they exist, are often related to the musher—a spouse, sibling, or parent. Handlers help with training and dog maintenance. They pack the gear, food, and supplies; make sure the truck is in working order; and put straw in the boxes. They literally follow the race in their trucks. (FDNM; photograph by Mike Belrose.)

To keep warm in a region where temperatures can dip to minus 60 degrees Fahrenheit (not counting the windchill factor), mushers wear several layers of clothing. Musher Hano Oeltler is wearing two warm inner layers covered by an Eskimo-style anorak/parka with a wolf ruff (which keeps frost from obscuring his vision). He wears otter-fur driving mitts over wool gloves. (YQA; photograph by Mary Shreves.)

At its most basic, mushing is the use of dog-powered transportation created by harnessing dogs to a sled via a gangline. The driver climbs on and yells, "Go!" or "All right!" or "Hike!"—but never "Mush!" "Mush!" is the mark of someone who has watched far too much television, and even the dogs will laugh at it. (YQA.)

Mercury and Crusher, Sonny Lindner's leaders, take a well-deserved rest at Eagle while waiting for Lindner to get straw for their bed. Mercury, hot from the exertion, sticks his snout in the snow to cool down. (FDNM; photograph by J. Correia.)

Jeff King crosses Eagle Summit, the gap named after the nearby Eagle River by prospectors from Circle City. This is a high-wind "convergence zone"—a meeting place between the Yukon Flats and Tanana Valley. Blowing snow is gritty and painful when it crashes against the skin. The crossing at Eagle Summit is a symmetrical saddle, with two high peaks separated by about 100 yards. The final slope is a 30-degree angle scoured down to bare rock and tundra due to the high, sandblasting winds. Mushers sometimes wrap their runners with chains as they descend to slow down the sled's momentum and prevent a disastrous rush to the bottom. (YQA.)

WHAT'S IN A NAME?

Eagle Summit, shown here in the summer, is a 3,652-foot gap through the White Mountains of central Alaska. An early explorer, Hudson Stuck, wrote in 1916: "The Eagle Summit is one of the most difficult summits in Alaska. The wind blows so fiercely that sometimes for days together its passage is almost impossible." (EM.)

In 1984, Mother Nature threw a howling blizzard out just to shake things up. Ice formed around the dogs' eyes and mushers' faces, so they could not see. The wind keened, piercing even the warmest furs and parkas, and got into their heads like a banshee on the prowl. Several mushers were no match for the wind, which was strong enough to knock down even the biggest mushers and their 300-pound sleds. Most mushers struggled through, but a few turned back to camp at the base in order to wait for better conditions. Both sleds and dogs took a beating, but no major injuries occurred. "I was scared," Bob English admitted. "The dogs were scared." (EM.)

In 1986, Don Glassburn was running about mid-pack, a bit out of Circle, when he met a team—without a musher—that was running the wrong way. Glassburn chased the team down and followed the trail, finding musher Ed Borden, who lost his sled when he got pinched between the sled and some ice on the river; Borden's leg was fractured. Glassburn bundled Borden into his own sled and headed back toward Circle, where he dropped Borden off. Glassburn did not think twice about this—he just did it, and he saved Borden's life. Glassburn returned to the race, considerably farther behind, and later won the Sportsmanship Award for his actions. (YQA.)

WHAT'S IN A NAME?

Since some of the race route crossed or paralleled recreational trails or active traplines, after the first race, the board added highly useful trail signs. During the inaugural race, several mushers lost their way more than once. (EM.)

Volunteer veterinarian Jean Buist (right) talks with musher Bill Cotter. A team of veterinarians at each checkpoint examines all dogs, and no dog is allowed to continue the race unless the vet team says it can. Dog care was, is, and always will be the overriding concern of the race. (YQA; photograph by Roger D. Williams.)

The dogs took on a frosty look as temperatures that dropped to minus 50 degrees Fahrenheit combined with warm humid air at Arctic Circle Hot Springs, creating a frosty white coating on almost everything. This section, which crosses frozen swamps and streams, is known for its incredible cold. Everyone waited nervously for the first teams to arrive during that first race. When a local pilot reported seeing a team on the Steese Highway at noon, they were skeptical—as that was fast—and when it was verified and an additional team spotted, they got ready. After 15 hours on the trail, Joe Runyan swung into the checkpoint late Sunday night, and cheers broke out. The tension—so high it buzzed—began to dissipate. Runyan received a silver coin for being the first to reach checkpoint no. 2 first, but he shrugged off the honor; he was too busy thanking his team for bringing him along so quickly. Sonny Lindner followed about an hour later on a "sit-down" sled, which sparked numerous jokes about "saddle sores." There was laughter as Lindner pulled in, but he ignored it as he checked his dogs. (FDNM; photograph by Mike Mathers.)

Harry Sutherland arrived at Circle Hot Springs with a damaged sled. He rested a few hours but hurried to Circle, where he was able to repair his sled and get on with the race. He spent much of the race concerned about one of his dogs, which seemed to have injured a foot. (FDNM; photograph by J. Correia.)

Veterinarian Karl Monetti checks Sutherland's dog Roar, while the musher looks on. The vet diagnosed a sore foot, recommending "a good rest." (FDNM; photograph by J. Correia.)

WHAT A LOAD!

Mushers are allowed to use only one sled or toboggan during the entire race. A large sled will be required as the mushers are required to carry:

1. Proper cold weather sleeping bag
2. Hand ax with a handle over 22" long
3. One pair of standard, 36" minimum length snow shoes with bindings
4. Official promotional materials
5. Eight booties for each dog
6. Map and compass
7. Food Requirements allow for 3 lbs. of dog food for each dog for each 50 miles of the race:
   Fairbanks — 5 lbs. per dog
   Chena Hot Springs — 5 lbs. per dog
   Circle Hot Springs — 5 lbs. per dog
   Circle City — 15 lbs. per dog
   Eagle — 10 lbs. per dog
   Dawson — 25 lbs. per dog
   Carmacks — 10 lbs. per dog

Mushers will also be carrying many of the following items: coveralls, mittens, parka, tether line, cookstove, dog dishes, thermos bottle, extra boots, gaiters, headlamp, batteries, matches, face mask, first aid kit, foot ointment, sewing kit, repair kit, bolts, screws, snaps, tent, and lunch.

Each musher may start with a maximum number of 12 dogs. Only three dogs may be dropped during the race and a musher cannot run fewer than five dogs. Dogs will be left at designated dog drops, but they must get to the dog drop in harness or in the sled.

Each musher will spend a mandatory 36 hours in Dawson. The differences in the starting times (they start at 2 minute intervals) will be made up at this time. The teams will be leaving Dawson with the heaviest load they will carry during the race. There will be 25 lbs. of dog food in the sled for each dog.

Only the mushers can handle and feed the dogs during the race. They are also responsible for keeping the trail clear when they set up camp and for cleaning up before they take off. There is a possible $500 fine for littering.

The only drug that can be used in the dogs will be a topical foot ointment. Dogs will be tested before and during the race for prohibited drugs. Any dog that requires drugs must be dropped from the race.

The Race Marshall, Carl Huntington, will have the final word in making decisions concerning the Official Rules.

Because the trail was so rough and there was so much space between checkpoints, LeRoy Shank and the board knew mushers who were not prepared would run into trouble, and trouble can lead to death in this environment. To avoid fatalities, Shank and the board came up with a list of certain equipment and amounts of food every musher had to carry throughout the race, because this is a dangerous land for the unprepared. The sleds are checked before the start and at each checkpoint; mushers are fined, penalized, or even disqualified if they are missing anything on the list. (Shank.)

WHAT'S IN A NAME?

Extra harnesses and snowshoes are among required equipment mushers must carry. Mushers who are not prepared for rough trails and inclement weather can run into trouble, and trouble can lead to death in this environment. Competition can cloud judgment. Even the most dedicated dog man or woman could be blinded by the urge to win—sometimes, with the eye on the prize, the feet stumble. A musher might overestimate his or her abilities, omitting something vital to lighten the load. (YQA.)

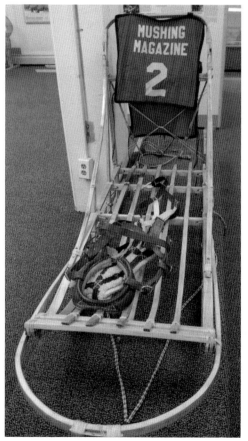

The most important piece of equipment is the sled. Sleds have to be sturdy, because they take a beating over the course of 1,000 miles. Mushers become handymen of sorts, who are able to fix anything. They carry extra parts and learn to replace and repair every single inch of their conveyances. (EM.)

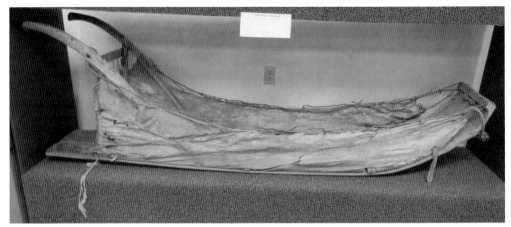

The traditional Athabaskan toboggan is the favored sled design in the Yukon Territory. Constructed of handworked wood, with moose hide on the front and sides, this toboggan was preferred over runners in soft, deep snow. This sled, the property of Interior trapper Fabian Cary, was purchased in Fort Yukon, probably around 1920, and loaned to the Fairbanks Community Museum by Peter Bowers of Fairbanks. (Bob Eley.)

Dog boxes do not have to be huge, just big enough for the dogs to lie down comfortably. A large opening is usually covered with wire mesh so dogs cannot remove it. Straw on the floor keeps the animals warm. (Shank.)

WHAT'S IN A NAME?

6

BROKEN DREAMS
AND ROUSING CHEERS

There are as many reasons for scratching as there are mushers and races. Illness, injury, lack of gear, bad conditions, bad luck—every year, unexpected events test the hardiest of souls.

Losing a dog to illness or injury can dishearten mushers—and the rest of the team—to the point that their heads are no longer in the race. Sleep deprivation does not help. Inclement weather can demoralize a musher. Sometimes, it is the team that quits. If the team will not go any further, there is no use shouting or clubbing them into submission. Huskies are stubborn: they will go until they drop, but if they decide they do not want to run any more, they will not run any more.

Scratching is an agonizing decision, mushers admit. They have spent thousands of hours and dollars, and, more importantly, they have invested in their hopes and dreams for years. They have sacrificed much for this obsession, and their families and friends have sacrificed, too. However, it is better to quit the race than continue out of a sense of pride and end up killing a dog or themselves. Mushers often wait until the last possible minute, because when the decision is made, it is done—there is no going back into the race.

On Monday, Jack Stevens was the first musher to scratch; after catching a little bug from his dogs outside Fairbanks, he just could not keep going. However, he was more worried about his dogs than himself, saying, "I don't like to see my dogs sick." John Two Rivers scratched out of Chena Hot Springs due to injured leaders and an unwilling team.

Scratching is not the end of the world. The Yukon Quest is a tough race. Simply starting—making the attempt—is more than most people will ever do. If a virus runs through a team, or the dogs sour, the musher really has no choice. Musher illness is another reason to scratch—since most mushers are already sleep-deprived, adding an illness is guaranteed to make finishing impossible. Of the 26 teams that started in 1984, six scratched before reaching Whitehorse; two made it to Dawson City before making the difficult decision to withdraw from the race.

There were success stories, too, and reasons for the crowd to cheer that first year. Kevin Turnbough, who arrived with his team looking strong, mentioned the winds and how much of a struggle it was going over Eagle Summit. Lorrina Mitchell arrived tired but smiled graciously and answered questions from bystanders, particularly children who were excited to be out of school for a few minutes to witness history in the making. The crowd gave its loudest cheers for hometown hero Don Glassburn. He would love to sign all the kids' programs, he told the crowd, but not right now. His team was skittish because of the noise and excitement, and he really wanted to keep going.

Wilson Sam slid in with a sad tale—he flipped his sled on Eagle Summit, losing his dog food pans and booties. Quest rules required a certain number of booties to protect the dogs' feet, and Sam was sure it spelled the end of his race. But word went out from Circle Hot Springs, and when Sam arrived in Central, several women had set up a sewing circle and made 92 pairs of booties almost overnight; they also scrounged up some pans for food.

When a dog is ill or injured on the trail, it is secured in a sled bag until the team arrives at the next dog drop where a handler can pick it up. Mushers can drop dogs for any reason, though they must maintain the minimum number of dogs (five) to finish the race. (YQA.)

In 1987, Jon Gleason scratched at 101 Mile Steese Highway, in minus 60 degrees Fahrenheit temperatures, because he did not dress warmly enough to battle the chilling winds between Eagle and Circle City. He suffered cracked and bleeding hands and burned cheeks; he dropped when one of his dogs got a frozen front paw. (FDNM/YQA; photograph by Charles Mason.)

BROKEN DREAMS AND ROUSING CHEERS

Most mushers transport their teams in dog boxes, which are large wooden boxes typically tailored to the size of a truck bed and divided into sections for the dogs. Many have areas for equipment and sleds. Boxes are installed on pickup trucks for travel to practice and races. (YQA.)

Excited villagers and schoolchildren, witnessing history, met the mushers at each checkpoint. If a musher happened to be from that town, the entire town usually turned out to cheer for the hometown hero. (FDNM.)

A team waits (somewhat) patiently for an exam at the vet check. Volunteer veterinarians and vet techs check each team before the race. Some mushers bring one or two more dogs than they plan to run, because only dogs at the official check can start; this provides options if a planned racer becomes ill. (EM.)

Veterinarian Dr. Bruce Lee is pictured in 1984. The race veterinarians are volunteers recruited from Alaska and Canada. At the checkpoints, they examine each dog for injuries, illness, stress, dehydration, or general malaise, and then quiz the mushers on the team's performance or any unusual happenings. (YQA; photograph by Roger D. Williams.)

Volunteers Bob Goodwin (left), Randy Navin (center), and Joe Galvin assemble posts that will hold the banner for the Yukon Quest starting line on the frozen Chena River in Fairbanks. Without volunteers, the first race never would have gotten past the dreaming stage. Without volunteers, nothing gets done. "You couldn't pay people to work like that," LeRoy Shank said. "Nobody working for money would work that hard." Organizing and putting on a race is vastly different from running in one. Those who focused on raising money forgot other aspects of the race, and those focusing on the race forgot that it takes money to run it. Everyone was off in his or her own world with tunnel vision. "It's like a hungry dog with 10 dishes of dog food," said Shank, in an analogy, "it will run from dish to dish, but it won't eat. The ultimate goal is to eat, but there's so much going on here I can't eat, or I'll keep it covered so nobody else gets it." Yet Shank knew the group's strength was its vision—the race was the priority. "We literally had fistfights in that office because people would disagree on things, but . . . the race is going to win out over personality," Shank recalled. (FDNM; photograph by Kathi Berry.)

When the mushers arrived in Circle, the snow had started falling, so everyone set up camp and waited it out. No one wanted to be the first to leave and, thus, the trailbreaker. Trail-breaking is hard work; it tires the dogs, expends more calories, and slows the pace. Mushers care deeply for their dogs, and the first real tragedy of the Yukon Quest had occurred on Wednesday, just before the mushers reached Eagle. Although dog care is the top priority during the race, harsh conditions and the hellish climate can take a toll on both man and beast. One of Nick Ericson's dogs stopped running, lying down in his harness. Ericson stopped the sled to check him, intending to put the dog in the sled and carry it on to the next checkpoint. Alas, the dog died in his arms. Ericson was devastated and lay down next to the dog. In these conditions, this could have led to a second tragedy were it not for Kevin Turnbough, who came upon the distraught musher and his team a few minutes later. Turnbough, well-versed in dealing with grief and pain, used his ministerial training and skills to convince Ericson to get up and keep going. (FDNM.)

BROKEN DREAMS AND ROUSING CHEERS

A sign marks the end of the Steese Highway at Circle City. According to legend, this city got its name because its founder thought he had reached the Arctic Circle, which is actually 50 miles north. (EM.)

Crabb's Corner in Central, a bar, restaurant, convenience store, and motel owned and operated by Jim and Sandy Crabb from 1982 to 2002, stayed open 24/7 during the first race. Joe Runyan was the first to arrive at Crabb's; he left quickly and arrived in Circle City later that evening. (EM.)

Areas of open water, or leads, are prevalent along the Yukon, even in the winter. In these spots, it is easy to break through into the water, and wet skin freezes very quickly. Even dogs can die from exposure if their paws and fur get wet. In situations like this, the only smart thing to do is immediately stop, start a fire, and quickly dry all the dogs. Otherwise, a musher is courting frostbite and death. Bob English had a close call in a lead, but his dogs managed to pull the sled out of the water. English stopped immediately, started a fire, and dried everybody. The incident made him more careful; later, when he heard water flowing (it was too dark to see), he stopped and found the open lead in the ice—his team was heading right for it. Disaster was averted. English labored into the hot springs on Tuesday; he regaled the crowd with a wild tale of struggle and survival, but he was not exaggerating much. Crowd favorite Mary Shields, however, interrupted his stories with her arrival. Meanwhile, Joe Runyan had left in minus 20 degrees Fahrenheit temperatures. Runyan took the lead, but it was too soon to predict who would win the inaugural Yukon Quest. (FDNM.)

BROKEN DREAMS AND ROUSING CHEERS

The Yukon River (pictured here at Circle City) is the third-longest river in North America, flowing 1,980 miles from British Columbia to the Bering Sea. It has a total drainage area of 321,500 square miles and was the major transportation route for gold-seekers during the Klondike gold rush from 1896 to 1903. (EM.)

Jeff King feeds his dogs at Central, an unofficial checkpoint. Checkpoints are set up with drop bags, straw, a musher station, a media staging area, and more. Areas for mushers to use as bed-down stations require a large space for a sled, 12 dogs, and a big handler truck. (FDNM; photograph by Charles Mason.)

In 1984, it took time for the Yukon River to firmly freeze on the stretch into Eagle. It was a ragged obstacle course of broken ice chunks jumbled into piles, called pack ice or "jam ice." Historically, miners and would-be fortune-seekers traveled the river, called the "Highway of the North," via boat during the summer and dog sled in the winter. The native Yupik called the river Kwiguk, meaning "large stream." "Yukon" is the Gwich'in word for "great river." In its circuitous route from near the Gulf of Alaska to the Bering Sea, the Yukon River meanders—sometimes faltering,

sometimes bold—like the men who followed its path to the goldfields. Crossings for the 1984 race were essentially the same crossings used since the gold rush, because they were in the places where the ice is easier (less jumbled). Of course, it is never an easy ride—overflow, ice piles, glare ice, glassy ice, frozen sinkers (tree trunks or stumps that float down the river, getting frozen in the ice when the river freezes up), slushy spots during warm weather, open leads—all of these can lead to slow going or even disaster if a musher is not paying attention. (YQA.)

Jumble ice occurs when ice on a river or other flowing body of water fractures due to different flow rates beneath the ice. On a lake, pond, or other stationary body of water, ice forms undisturbed and generally does not move as long as the entire surface of the body of water is frozen. When a river freezes, water flow typically continues beneath the ice, exerting pressure on it. If the ice fractures, pieces of ice torn free by the river's current will collide with stationary or slower-moving pieces. After becoming stuck in place, the loosened pieces of ice refreeze irregularly, causing a rough, or jumbled, surface. In general, the faster a body of water flows beneath ice, the more likely it is to develop jumble ice. Temperatures near the freezing point also tend to cause jumble ice, as higher temperatures weaken the ice structure, allowing for more pieces to be torn free before refreezing. Jumble ice is a hazard for winter travelers, as the broken "ground" formed by it can cause damage to sleds or injuries to dogs. (FDNM; photograph by Charles Mason.)

Long, bare stretches of ice blown by wind into glass-smooth flatness can cause a heavy sled to slide across the ice with no way to stop if it makes a sudden move or is hit with sudden gusts of wind, which are common in this part of the world. (YQA.)

A tired reporter grabs forty winks at Crabb's Corner. As soon as the first musher comes in, the press people run out for interviews, and then all want access at the same time to get their stories. Meanwhile, the Yukon Quest has its own media team also trying to send out news. (FDNM.)

The race route is a landscape of alpine tundra and boreal forest. The trail runs along frozen rivers. The 49-mile stretch between Circle City and Eagle can be dangerous, with high winds and blowing snow that covers trail markers. It is a very cold section, with temperatures sinking far below zero as the cold air sinks from the mountains to the bottom of the river valley. Eagle, the location of checkpoint no. 4, was incorporated in 1901 as the first "city" in Alaska. It is "off the road system," meaning that unless the river is frozen, the only way to get to Eagle is by airplane or boat. As Eagle awaited the reamaining 24 teams on Thursday, the smell of salmon pot pie and hot coffee wafted through the air. Race officials watched the snow falling. LeRoy Shank saw the first team way out across the ice, and yelled, "Dog team!" Chaos ensued. Down below Eagle Bluff, the tiny team seemed to grow larger as it came closer. Someone yelled for the bell at St. John's Episcopal Church to ring, so checkpoint manager Steve Nelson grabbed the rope and pulled for all he was worth, shaking the steeple in his enthusiasm. The bell tolled, letting everyone know

BROKEN DREAMS AND ROUSING CHEERS

the first team was coming. Details were shouted as people could identify them—the color of the sled bag, the number of dogs, the color of the parka. "Must be Sonny [Lindner]," whispered the crowd at the sight of a red sled bag. As the sled disappeared below the bank of the Yukon River and then reappeared, it became clear: Lindner was the first musher to hit Eagle. Shank remembers that the sun broke out just as Lindner came to a stop in front of the church, the golden sunlight lighting his blond hair. "It brought tears to my eyes," Shank recalled, unashamed. It was a touching moment—the moment he realized his dream had finally come true. Members of the crowd asked Lindner, "How do you feel?" "I feel good," Lindner said, "the dogs feel good." The front-runners arrived within 15 minutes of each other, followed a mere 12 hours later by a second group that included Bill Cotter. In a race of that distance, 12 hours is nothing, Cotter said, "you're still a long ways from nowhere this far into the race." (YQA.)

In 1874, trader Moses Mercer established Belle Isle as a trading post. It was the main rest stop for Yukon River highway traffic between Interior Alaska and the Klondike and became a mining camp in 1889. Belle Isle was renamed Eagle City for a 300-foot-high bluff populated by bald eagles. Now called just Eagle, it is the only checkpoint not accessible by road. (FDNM.)

Mushers and handlers sit inside the Eagle checkpoint drying wet clothing, having hot coffee, and spending a few minutes checking in. Although the mushers are very competitive during the race, most are good friends and enjoy visiting, even when they are trying to beat each other. (FDNM.)

Jeff King is pictured in downtown Eagle. Winter visitors are rare in the villages along the Yukon River, so the Quest was eagerly anticipated. Eagle announced each team's arrival with the toll of the St. John's Episcopal Church bell, a signal to the mushers that the journey from Circle was at an end. (YQA.)

A musher leaves Eagle and heads for Dawson City loaded down with supplies and gear. For the next 95 miles, the musher and his/her team will encounter some of the harshest, most inhospitable climates and conditions on the planet; it helps to have plenty of food, good gear, and tough dogs. (FDNM.)

The Northern Commercial Company is pictured sometime between 1909 and 1916. Eagle, established as a Northern Commercial Company trading post in 1874, was the main rest stop for Yukon River traffic between Alaska and the Klondike and the transportation hub for miners from the Yukon River and tributaries. A telegraph line was built in 1903; Roald Amundsen wired notice of his successful Northwest Passage expedition from Eagle in 1905. (Frank and Frances Carpenter Collection, Library of Congress, gift of Mrs. W. Chapin Huntington; 1951/public domain.)

Sonny Lindner was a veteran distance racer, so he had stops down to a science. Here, he spreads straw for his team at the Yukon River village of Eagle. Lindner was the first musher to arrive at this remote checkpoint off the road system. (FDNM; photograph by J. Correia.)

Harry Sutherland stops several miles outside Eagle to snack his dogs before starting up the hill. It is a dilemma faced by every musher: how much can the dogs run before they sour? If they are run too hard, they will not start again; if they are stopped too soon, it may ruin their flow. (FDNM; photograph by J. Correia.)

Racing dogs learn to sleep anywhere and anytime, knowing that sleep is not scheduled and must be grabbed when it is most convenient. When it's nap time, most huskies will curl up into tight balls, noses tucked into their bushy tails, and fall asleep immediately. (FDNM; photograph by Brian O'Donoghue.)

Volunteers handle most aspects of the race. They check sleds, man checkpoints, assist media, assist veterinarians, make sure only authorized people are in the staging areas, track teams, man the office, plan and assist with events, sell merchandise, provide security, assist mushers, and hang on to enthusiastic teams. Volunteers come from Fairbanks, Canada, and the Lower 48. (EM.)

Jeff King puts booties on his dogs before leaving a checkpoint. Small, sock-shaped booties, made of heavy cotton or fleece with Velcro fasteners, protect a dog's feet from rough trails, ice, roadways, or trails with no snow. (FDNM.)

BROKEN DREAMS AND ROUSING CHEERS

The Fortymile River, so called by prospectors because it joins the Yukon River about 40 miles from Canada's Fort Reliance, cut into bedrock for millions of years as the surrounding region experienced earthquakes, uplifting, and faulting, which created the awe-inspiring Dawson Bluffs, toweing over the musher. The river's inexorable movement left its mark in the gravel river terraces overlooking the river from some 800 feet above the water. Gold was left in the gravel after washing down from the metamorphic rocks exposed when the river cut through the bedrock. The river has close to 17 forks and offshoots and travels 392 miles through the state of Alaska. (FDNM.)

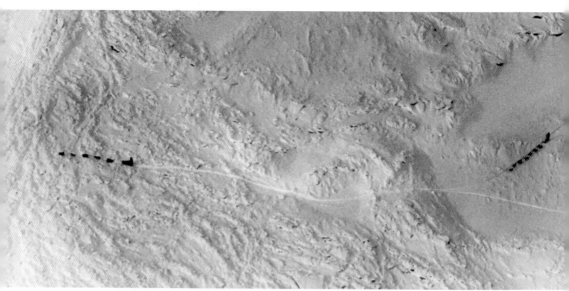

Two mushers traverse the frozen Yukon River about 35 miles outside of Dawson City. All mushers were required to lay over for 36 hours in Dawson City to give themselves and their dogs a chance to rest and recuperate. In 1984, some of the mushers banded together during a horrendous storm, cooperating so all arrived safely. The snow made it difficult to tell where river ended and bank began and where ice ended and water began. The mushers formed a band across the river, shouting to each other and letting one another know when they found the right path—a musher's version of the popular water game Marco Polo. When darkness fell, they stopped to camp, choosing safety over the race. Jeff King told reporters it was because they got lost. When the sun rose, the mushers found the trail, which was about 0.12 miles from their campsite. (FDNM; photograph by J. Correia.)

BROKEN DREAMS AND ROUSING CHEERS

A team pulls into Dawson City, founded when prospector Robert Henderson staked a 160-acre townsite and built a store on the only available land after George Carmack made the Bonanza Creek strike. The town was named after George Mercer Dawson, who served as director of the Geological and Natural History Survey of Canada from 1895 to 1901. Dawson City was a raw, frontier town—dirty, loud, and dangerous, with lots of saloons, lots of excitement, little hygiene, and the resulting typhoid. By 1899, there were approximately 40,000 people in town, but they were mostly gone by 1900, when the nearby gold claims had been exhausted. Most people had left for the Klondike by this time. Food and supplies were short, and only the strongest, hardiest, and most committed folks stayed—a situation similar to the one faced by Yukon Quest racers in 1984. Dawson City was the capital of the Yukon Territory until 1951, when the capital was moved to Whitehorse. This section of the race was cobbled together from the Overland Trail and numerous trapline trails. Trappers often set traps close to trails; in the true spirit of the North, many area trappers pulled their traps, giving up considerable income to show their enthusiastic support for the race, and some helped break and groom the trail. This area is still a harsh, rugged land. (FDNM; photograph by Charles Mason.)

In this image, the racers make camp in Dawson City. This is the only checkpoint where mushers are allowed assistance with their teams. Handlers take on dog care and feeding while mushers rest and find ways to lighten their 300-pound loads to gain extra speed for the latter half of the race. (YQA; photograph by Roger D. Williams.)

Mushers, checkers, handlers, and other volunteers and officials huddle around a fire sled set up in the middle of the checkpoint area. To make a fire sled, a 55-gallon drum is bolted to sled runners, creating a portable fire pit. (FDNM; photograph by J. Correia.)

Bob England makes repairs to his dog sled in Dawson City. Mushers take the layover opportunity to rest: they run on adrenaline, little food, and even less sleep. Sleep-deprived humans make mistakes, and this is country that does not forgive mistakes; a simple error can lead to a cascade of failures that could result in injury or death for dog and/or man. (YQA; photograph by Roger D. Williams.)

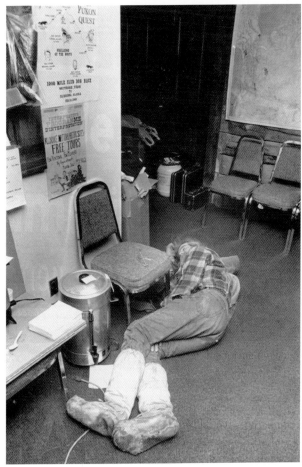

A musher grabs a corner of the checkpoint floor for a nap. It can be difficult to sleep in the chaotic conditions of the checkpoint. With so many people wandering about, the sounds of footfalls, talking, rustling, and snoring are almost overwhelming. Tired mushers—like their dogs—learn to sleep anywhere. (FDNM; photograph by Brian O'Donoghue.)

By Sunday night, everyone had checked in to Dawson City except Shirley Liss. Darryle Adkins was the second musher to lose a dog; it died in harness just outside Dawson City, and Adkins scratched. Bob English thought about scratching, but other mushers talked him out of it. "Wait until the rest period is over," they counseled. "See how the dogs are after they've had some sleep and care." After catching up on sleep, the mushers went over their strategies, tweaking plans, changing things as they assessed conditions and anticipated future ones. Often, winning is not a matter of dogs or equipment; it is how one's mind runs the race. Successful mushers are observant, watching everything. They learn from past mistakes and remember and incorporate winning moves and ideas. Musher personality also determines what type of race he or she will run. While no musher will admit to a "plan," the good ones usually have a general idea of what they will do. They know that nothing in a long-distance race ever goes as planned, so they have backups and

BROKEN DREAMS AND ROUSING CHEERS

contingencies and are ready for anything. Flexibility is vital; rigidity will lead to death for the musher or a dog. Since this was the first year of the race, the racers—with sparse knowledge of the trail and rapidly changing weather conditions—concentrated on keeping their teams healthy and not damaging their sleds. After Dawson City, however, mushers switched focus, stopping less frequently and for shorter periods of time. In Dawson City, Joe Runyan found himself a poke of gold richer for being the first racer into checkpoint no. 5, the halfway mark. The mushers got some much-needed rest and relaxation, letting their handlers and others do the grunt work. The citizens of this historic gold rush town, always known for providing a good time, rolled out the welcome mat for the Yukon Quest mushers much as their ancestors may have during the Klondike gold rush in 1898. (FDNM.)

The dogs rested well in Dawson City, basking in the warm winter sunshine. A balmy temperature of near zero degrees made the layover seem like a tropical vacation to some. (FDNM.)

BROKEN DREAMS AND ROUSING CHEERS

7

HALFWAY TO WHITEHORSE AND BEYOND

Bob English checked his dogs again on Monday, after they had rested for 36 hours, and decided scratching from the race was in their best interest. English had a team of really young dogs that, he reasoned, gave it their all and had nothing left; there was always next year.

After the mandatory rest, mushers began leaving Dawson City at one-hour intervals determined by their arrival times at the halfway point. The 36-hour layover was extended by about an hour for each musher in order to make up for the staggered start in Fairbanks a week earlier.

Joe Runyan was the first musher out of Dawson City. As the sun rose, he mushed out of the city onto the Yukon River. Runyan would be breaking the trail for those who left later, the guys who wanted to beat him into Whitehorse—Jeff King, Harry Sutherland, Bill Cotter, and Sonny Lindner. Dogs that have to break trail expend more calories for fewer results. Runyan realized his error before he left, telling a reporter, "This is the stupidest thing I've ever done in my life."

Lindner and Runyan traded the lead after Dawson City; Lindner took it on Tuesday, as the trail dropped down to the Indian River. Runyan was the odds-on favorite, but Lindner made a push after Dawson City, knowing he had an advantage with his dogs. "They were still pretty fat," Lindner said of his team. "Joe's were looking thin," meaning he would have to stop more often to feed them.

Gerald Riley, Ron Aldrich, Kevin Turnbough, Jack Hayden, and Senley Yuill traveled together. They camped on the Yukon River, piling spruce boughs onto the ice. After the Black Hills, Riley left the group to make a run for the lead. Even though they were fierce competitors who each wanted that first-place finish, Runyan, Lindner, Cotter, Sutherland, and King were also friends—camping together at night and enjoying the company—until Lindner made his move on Wednesday. "We all camped together until we got in the Black Hills," Lindner said. "Then I got itchy and took off."

As the trail crossed the Stewart River, Lindner kept the lead. He got a bit concerned, however, after camping for about six hours without seeing any other team. Thinking he had possibly taken a wrong turn, he went back until he ran into Sutherland at a fork in the road.

Bruce Johnson caught everyone by surprise when he made a big push for the finish, pulling up to sixth place. Lindner went through Minto Landing in the Yukon just before noon; then the weather got ugly, meaning less cold—warm weather softens the trail, making it "punchy," and the dogs easily overheat. Lindner slowed down, and all the mushers on the trail stopped to camp and wait for the cooler evening to arrive.

Geologically, this area did not experience the rough and tumble of volcanic deformation 100 million years ago; erosion contributed to its flat-topped and rounded hills. This was the area where teams could go all-out, put on a burst of speed, and pick up the pace. Mushers who had run the race gently so far, keeping some strength in reserve, had an advantage.

This 1899 bird's-eye view of Dawson City shows the Yukon River in the foreground. At the height of the gold rush, Dawson City suffered severe food shortages, leading Canadian authorities to decree that anyone coming in had to have one year's worth of supplies. They checked everyone at the top of the Chilkoot Pass, and preparation often required numerous trips up and down the dreaded pass to stockpile enough supplies. (Copyright by Pillsbury & Cleveland Co., No. 34.)

A musher's handler learns to sleep anywhere, in any conditions, whenever there is time. Since mushers are allowed to have assistance in Dawson City, most take advantage; the handlers spend most of the time working while the musher rests. (FDNM; photograph by Mike Belrose.)

At camp near Dawson City, a sleeping dog is covered by a burlap sack once used to carry feed. Veterinarians checked each dog, looking at feet, pads, joints, muscles, and eyes. They rubbed salve into cracked foot pads and massaged tender joints and wrists. Dogs ate plenty of high-fat food in order to build their strength. (YQA; photograph by Mike Belrose.)

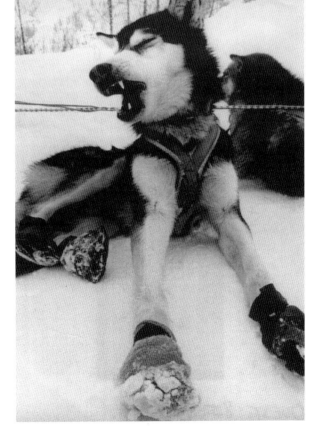

A tired, bootied Rags, from Joe Runyan's team, yawns as he waits for attention at the Dawson City checkpoint. Mushers remove booties while the dogs sleep to avoid cutting off circulation in the dogs' feet. (FDNM; photograph by V. DeWitt.)

Sonny Lindner (right) is pictured at the Dawson City sled repair area. Race rules limited mushers to one sled for the entire race. A musher needs basic sled repair skills and equipment, because it is a rough trail, and trees, rocks, ice, and other hazards are punishing. (YQA.)

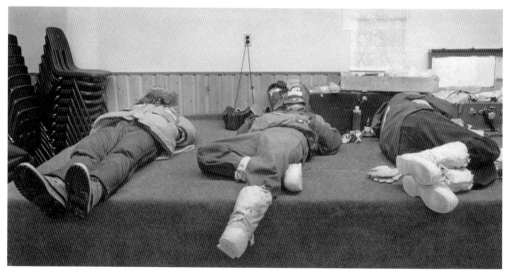

A handler (right) and two veterinarians catch a nap while waiting for mushers at Carmacks. Family members make great handlers. Some racers offer budding mushers a handling job before sponsoring them in a big race, offering valuable experience and mentoring (not to mention dogs) to up-and-comers. (FDNM; photograph by Nora Gruner.)

Jeff King does some pre-race training at Takhini River. Old-timers say it takes roughly 3,000 to 5,000 miles of training to prepare a team for a long-distance race. (FDNM.)

Harry Sutherland's sled shows wear during the race. Sleds and teams have to contend with rocks, stumps, and trees, while trails with no snow and jumble ice also contribute to the battering. (FDNM; photograph by Charles Mason.)

Noise, crowds, or other distractions do not bother veteran race dogs; they sit or lie calmly, taking advantage of the rest and grabbing a short nap. (FDNM; photograph by Charles Mason.)

8

HAZARDS MOUNTING TO THE END OF THE LINE

It was unseasonably warm—so warm that the fast trail became too soft, and officials began mulling a change in route to bypass soft spots. The stretch of trail just before Braeburn was of concern. There was no snow, according to local mushers, and the trail wound around a mountain in a narrow ribbon barely wide enough for a single sled. The Klondike Highway was also very worrying; it is an active road with large vehicles rushing by at high speeds. Soft ice on the Yukon River and Lake Laberge added to the hazards, making conditions "a disaster waiting to happen," according to race marshal Carl Huntington.

For safety reasons, officials decided to truck the teams from Carmacks to Fox Lake, bypassing about 13 miles of snowless, rocky trail and the hazardous Klondike Highway. To accommodate the change, officials expanded the layover at Carmacks from four hours to seven, affording time to move the teams to the end of Fox Lake where the trail leaves the road.

Sonny Lindner pulled into checkpoint no. 6, Carmacks, after burning up the 290 miles of trail out of Dawson City; the Black Hills did not slow him at all. From Carmacks on, the race was between Lindner and Joe Runyan, who ran neck and neck with nine dogs each through the heavily forested hills dubbed "Pinball Alley" because of the rough terrain—sleds and teams are bounced around, jolting the drivers and freaking the dogs.

On Thursday, March 8, volunteers in Whitehorse scrambled to contact handlers and local residents to assist with the transport of the teams. It was a "madhouse," according to Wendy Waters. Local radio stations broadcast the news, and a fleet of trucks was dispatched to the checkpoint to help. The mushers supported Huntington's decision, which made everything much easier than it could have been.

Hundreds poured into Whitehorse to see the historic finish; the streets were jammed several people deep. The finish line was on First Avenue, and everyone waited for Lindner to swoop in and claim the purse. Lindner crossed the finish line at 1:20 p.m. on March 8, 1984. Spectators cheered when the winner, sunburned and exhausted, raced into town framed by a bright sky. He wore mirrored sunglasses that hid his eyes and carried a toothbrush in his mouth. Lindner finished with all his dogs. They pranced down the street, heads high and tails wagging.

Lorrina Mitchell almost did not cross the finish line—on March 9, she was nearly swept under the ice on the river just a mile from the finish. "It would be really disgusting to drown within sight of Whitehorse after surviving all the other ridiculous stuff I've been through," Mitchell said.

Legend has it that Senley Yuill and Ron Aldrich were met at the finish by their wives, who were wearing fur parkas; when the ladies took off their jackets, they were both wearing bikinis.

Another legend describes Frank Turner and Wilson Sam traveling together from Fox Lake until they were about 100 yards from the finish. They stopped, drew a line in the snow, and raced each other to the finish line; Turner beat Sam by one minute.

Sonny Lindner crossed the finish line in Whitehorse on March 8 at 1:20 p.m. with a time of 12:2:06, making history as the first winner of the Yukon Quest. He pocketed $15,000. In his characteristically laconic manner, he answered media queries with short replies. Yes, he'd do it again, but "not today." No, he was not tired, "just a little warm." Plans for the money? "Pay bills." (FDNM/YQA; photograph by Eric Muehling.)

A team runs beside an active roadway. Besides the obvious danger of traveling on active roads with tractor-trailers and other large vehicles rushing by at high speeds, mushing on highways tears up dogs' feet and destroys sleds. It can also be toxic—sled dogs grab hydration on the run, scooping up snow in their mouths for water. When they run along highways, they also slurp down sand, gravel, and other materials used for traction. Officials decided to truck teams out of Carmacks, bypassing the worrisome Klondike Highway. (FDNM.)

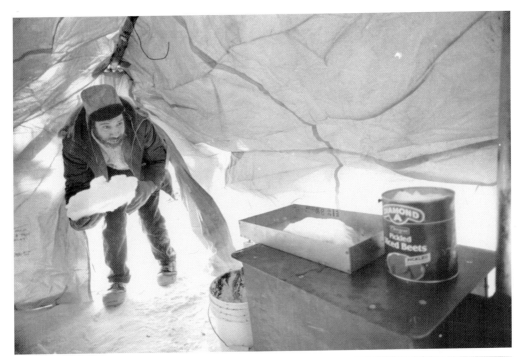

As he prepares to feed a team at Dawson City, handler Don Muller carries snow to be melted for water. Dawson City is the only checkpoint where handlers are allowed to assist the musher. (FDNM.)

Warmer temperatures not only softened the snow, they thinned the ice on Lake Laberge, making it dangerous for the teams and their fully loaded sleds. The finish line was moved to Carmacks for Shirley Liss, as the trail was too unsafe for her to go to Whitehorse. (FDNM; photograph by Mike Belrose.)

YUKON QUEST SLED DOG RACE

In 1984, the Yukon Quest finish line was at the White Pass & Yukon Route Railroad Depot, 120 miles from Carmacks. People lined up to witness the historic finish. (Shank.)

At the finish line in Whitehorse, people waited for hours for Lindner to arrive, knowing he left Carmacks first. Spectators watched the river for signs of his arrival, calling out false alarm after false alarm—in the Northern landscape, it can be easy to mistake a bush, rock, or critter for something else. (Shank.)

At 5:15 p.m., second-place finisher Harry Sutherland pulled into Whitehorse. Bill Cotter followed at 6:40 p.m.; Joe Runyan, who led most of the race, arrived after Cotter. Jeff King came in at 11:59 p.m., and Bruce Johnson was the first Canadian to finish, arriving at 7:07 p.m. on March 9. (Shank.)

Mushers were originally limited to 12 dogs per team and only allowed to drop three, with race organizers thinking mushers would be very careful about which dogs they took. This stipulation gave mushers with smaller kennels a chance to race competitively. Sonny Lindner won the first Yukon Quest without dropping any of his nine dogs. (Shank.)

Just before Whitehorse, the trail ran around fabled Lake Laberge, made famous by Robert Service in his poem "The Cremation of Sam McGee." The lake, which is 30 miles long and 1.2 to 3 miles wide, is a widening of the Yukon River north of Whitehorse. Its water is always very cold, and its weather is often harsh and suddenly variable. The Tagish knew it as Kluk-tas-si, and the Tlingit as Tahini-wud. It was named in commemoration of Robert de La Berge, one of the original colonists of New France (1658), and was well known to prospectors during the Klondike gold rush of the 1890s, as they passed Lake Laberge on their way to Dawson City. During the late 19th and early 20th centuries, after-winter steamers carrying goods on Lake Laberge early in the shipping season regarded the lake as trouble, since the ice was slow to thaw. The trail was confusing when the Quest mushers got to the lake. Snowmachine trails crisscrossing the frozen lake made it almost impossible to find the actual race trail, and almost every musher had to stop, knock on cabin doors, and ask residents how to get to Whitehorse. (FDNM.)

9

WE ARE ALL CHAMPIONS

The finish banquet was held in Whitehorse on Sunday, March 11. Mushers praised each other and the race organizers for a good race, which they all felt was "second to none."

Race marshal Carl Huntington was tasked with determining which musher displayed the best talent for Bush survival and "showed the greatest concern for the welfare of his or her team and best exemplified the spirit of the pioneer musher"—his choice, Senley Yuill, received a hand-crafted bronze Sourdough Award donated by mushing legend Joe May.

Joe Runyan's fellow mushers awarded him the Sportsmanship Trophy for his willingness to assist on the trail, even if it cost him his lead; the trophy was sponsored by MAPCO Petroleum.

"It's nice to get first," Runyan said, "and it is nice to cross the finish. But when you get something like this, it makes you want to keep competing. Whatever I did to get this, I hope that trend continues on in the future."

The Dawson gold poke went to Runyan, who arrived in Dawson City first *and* finished the race. The poke—which celebrates the halfway point of the grueling race, as well as a musher's safely getting to the Klondike and home—commemorates the history of the world's largest gold rush. It was sponsored by Kiwanis International. People who bet the first musher into Dawson will be the first across the finish line sometimes lose their shirts. Since the first race, only seven racers who were first into Dawson went on to become first-place finishers.

The biggest accomplishment, of course, is finishing and being able to hold bragging rights for that alone. To have taken the challenge—braving the extreme weather, harsh conditions, and tough course to get to the finish line in one piece—is an accomplishment very few people in the world can duplicate (the average scratch rate in the Yukon Quest is 35.5 percent).

The inaugural Yukon Quest officially ended on March 13 with the arrival of Shirley Liss, the Red Lantern finisher ("Red Lantern" being a nod to the tradition of leaving a light on for all mushers still on the trail). The Red Lantern trophy was sponsored by Sub-Arctic Mining. The finish line was moved to Carmacks because the trail had deteriorated on the Yukon River, making it unsafe. Liss crossed the line at 9:30 p.m. that night. Although she trailed the field throughout the race, Liss was satisfied with her run, saying she was making the trip, not competing.

Marti Steury called that first race a phenomenal success, praising the volunteers who worked many long hours and put it together. "When Sonny crossed the finish line, it was more than just the first musher to reach Whitehorse," Steury said. "Everybody that put anything into helping this race come off crossed the finish line with him."

LeRoy Shank's and Roger D. Williams's dream, so ephemeral at first, has become a reality known throughout the mushing world—and throughout the non-mushing world, as well—as a grueling, tough, challenging, adrenaline-inducing good ride. Not many men get to make a mark on the world, on history, on a sport. Shank and Williams got that chance, and they grabbed the brass ring without hesitation, putting in long, unpaid hours to see it come to fruition.

Jack Hayden, of Lake Minchumina, Alaska, was the eighth-place finisher. At the finish banquet, he told the crowd of 300 mushers, volunteers, officials, family, friends, and fans: "We finished our quest, and LeRoy finished his." (FDNM.)

A volunteer puts two dropped dogs into burlap bags for the trip home. If dogs are dropped in Eagle (the only place not on the road system), they are flown to the nearest checkpoint for retrieval by the handler. Handlers have access to every other checkpoint; dropped dogs spend the rest of the trip in familiar surroundings with someone they know. (FDNM.)

WE ARE ALL CHAMPIONS

The Yukon River freezes during the winter, but a large, long waterway does not stay static, and there were spots where the over-300-pound loads caused the ice to break. Breaking through into the water is dangerous when temperatures fall so low. (YQA; photograph by Charles Mason.)

These are the 1984 Yukon Quest race results. In the end, by all markers and measurements, the first Yukon Quest was an unparalleled success. The enduring appeal this race has for mushers from all over the world is apparent when, 30 years later, it attracts big-name mushers as well as new-to-the-sport contenders. Since that first race, the Quest has contained teams from Germany, France, Alaska, Canada, many states in the Lower 48, and other countries. Over 350 mushers have run the race—many more than once. (EM.)

Musher	Place	Time	Winnings	Hometown
Sonny Lindner	1	12:00:05	$15,000	Delta Junction
Harry Sutherland	2	12:05:15	$10,000	Delta Junction
Bill Cotter	3	12:05:40	$5,000	Nenana
Joe Runyan	4	12:07:51	$4,400	Tanana
Jeff King	5	12:10:59	$3,300	Denali Park
Bruce Johnson	6	12:18:07	$2,400	Atlin, BC
Gerald Riley	7	12:21:58	$1,900	Nenana
Jack Hayden	8	12:22:40	$1,500	Lake Minchumina
Kevin Turnbough	9	12:23:12	$1,400	Grand Marais, Minnesota
Pecos Humphrey	10	13:01:07	$1,000	Talkeetna
Lorrina Mitchell	11	13:03:08	$900	Whitehorse, Yukon
Senley Yuill	12	13:03:08	$800	Whitehorse, Yukon
Ron Aldrich	13	13:12:48	$700	Willow
Frank Turner	14	13:20:37	$600	Whitehorse, Yukon
Sam Wilson	15	13:20:38	$500	Huslia
Mary Shields	16	14:17:19		Schimmelpfenig Creek
Murray Clayton	17	14:17:23		Haines
Don Glassburn	18	14:23:55		Central
Nick Ericson	19	15:08:11		Fairbanks
Shirley Liss	20	No Time		Fairbanks
Daryle Adkins	S			Trapper Creek
Bob English	S			Whitehorse, Yukon
Dave Klumb	S			Fairbanks
Jack Stevens	S			Sunshine
Chris Whaley	S			College
John Two Rivers	S			North Pole

Regardless of which city hosts the finish, crossing the tape at the end of the "Toughest Sled Dog Race in the World" is no easy feat. Statistically, around 35.5 percent of starters do not finish the race. In the first 24 races, 776 teams started—only 513 finished. (Shank.)

The 1984 veterinary team consisted of Dr. Karin Schmidt, head veterinarian; Dr. Judy Harvey, at Chena Hot Springs; Dr. Karl Monetti, at Eagle; Dr. Val Stuve (pictured), at Carmacks; Dr. Leslie McDaniels, at Circle Hot Springs; Dr. Ken Kilpatrick and Dr. Patricia Smith, at Whitehorse; and Dr. Rollo Van Pelt, race pathologist. (YQA; photograph by Roger D. Williams.)

WE ARE ALL CHAMPIONS

An army of ham radio operators, such as Ken Klopf (pictured), donated time to broadcast news of the race round the clock. They kept tabs on the weather, passing along changes and warnings to checkpoints, at which handlers passed the information to mushers; this was especially important before the advent of the Internet, cell phones, and GPS. (YQA.)

In this 1898 image, an unending line of gold-seekers climbs the Chilkoot Pass toward the goldfields of the Klondike. By 1898, the rush had reached its peak. The White Star tram dropped about nine tons of freight an hour at the summit, and an estimated 30,000 people summited the pass. The first townsite was established in 1900 in a spot at the foot of the White Horse Rapids, named for the rapids' resemblance to the white manes of running horses. A post office was built soon after. (Copyright 1898 by E. A. Hegg.)

In 1984, most mushers were winging it throughout the race, with the most important element being the care of the dogs. Mushers concentrated on keeping teams strong and healthy and not losing their sleds to damage. After Dawson City, however, they switched their focus to driving, using the brakes a little less and stopping less frequently and for shorter periods of time. The one-sled rule and dog-drop limits even required distance-race veterans to rethink racing strategies. Mushers took much better care of their teams, as noticed by race officials like Leo Olesen, who remarked there were no "disposable dogs" in the race. (FDNM; photograph by Charles Mason.)

WE ARE ALL CHAMPIONS

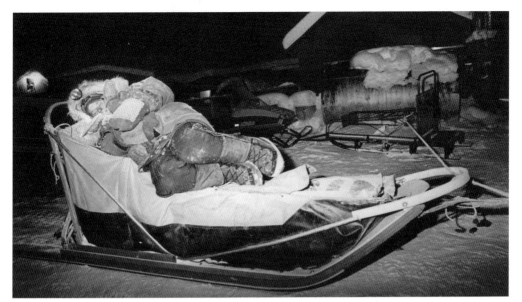

In this 1987 photograph, Jeff King takes a snooze at Crabb's Corner while the temperature is minus 57 degrees Fahrenheit. Although the Central Lodge offered hot meals and "free floor space" for naps, while Arctic Circle Hot Springs, the official checkpoint, offered a swimming pool, mineralized hot springs, and food, some mushers preferred quieter—albeit colder—accommodations. (YQA; photograph by Randy Belinsky.)

Mushers find novel ways to fund their obsession. If they are lucky, their local communities assist them. From left to right, Yukon Quest musher Don Glassburn, former executive director Lane St. John, fellow musher Jim Reighter, and supporter Rena Fleshman attend a fundraiser in Central. (FDNM/YQA; photograph by Ted Wilcox.)

Dr. Karin Schmidt of Fairbanks, the race's first head veterinarian, recruited eight colleagues. Dr. Schmidt earned her veterinary degree at Texas A&M; the call of the wild lured her to Alaska with her Volkswagen Beetle and a dog. She was notable for her "bunny boot ballet," a distinctly nonmedical dance performed behind the sled as she tried to keep her feet from freezing. (YQA; photograph by Roger D. Williams.)

Handler Gene Urning takes a short nap, along with one of his charges, as he waits for the mushers to arrive at a checkpoint. If a dog has to be dropped, just knowing a handler is there gives comfort to the musher. (FDNM.)

WE ARE ALL CHAMPIONS

Downtown Dawson City is pictured here in 1984. It is today the Yukon Territory's second-largest city. The territory is still a harsh, rugged land that is not easily traveled, especially in winter. (YQA; photograph by Roger D. Williams.)

Most Quest teams are mainly composed of Alaskan huskies, because these dogs have been bred to pull and run through grueling conditions. They are strong dogs with great endurance, well suited to the cold and harsh climate that serves as the Quest's backdrop. The Alaskan husky is defined by its purpose—pulling a sled as fast as possible. Even "pure" huskies have mixed ancestry, as early drivers bred for speed and endurance, not appearance or background. (Photograph by Carol Martin.)

This race is not about how fast a musher is or how much money he or she has, but about how well a musher takes care of the dogs and how well he or she can convince them to run 1,000 miles dragging a sled behind them. If a musher does not take care of the dogs, they will not take care of him or her, and if a sled dog decides it is not going to pull, nothing on earth can make it pull. (FDNM.)

WE ARE ALL CHAMPIONS

EPILOGUE

LeRoy Shank's only disappointment was not being able to run that first race. He had a very competitive team, but who had time to train? "It's my daughter," he said of the race, "But I couldn't. If I run the race, there's no race." Shank eventually ran in two subsequent races, taking 20th place in 1987 and scratching in 1990.

Eight of the 26 mushers who entered the first Yukon Quest International Sled Dog Race did not attempt it a second time. Darryle Adkins, Bob English, David Klumb, Jack Stevens, Chris Whaley, and John Two Rivers scratched for various reasons and never ran the trail again (at least not competitively). Senley Yuill, who placed 12th, and Wilson Sam, who placed 15th, also said farewell to a difficult and challenging trail.

Those who made multiple attempts had varying degrees of success. Frank Turner, the 14th-place finisher in 1984, started the race a record 23 times and crossed the finish line 18 times, taking first place in 1995. Jeff King, who ran the race seven times, took first place in 1989. Bill Cotter took his first-place win in 1987 and raced a total of five times; Bruce Johnson's 1986 first-place win capped a Quest career of four total races.

Sadly, Johnson's career ended in 1993. He placed second in the race after an astonishing sprint in the home stretch (pulling from fifth to second), but died that November when he and his team drowned after falling through thin ice while training on Little Atlin Lake. In 1994, Johnson was assigned bib no. 1 and honored with two minutes of silence at the start of the race.

Harry Sutherland ran the Quest for three more years, but never beat his second-place finish. Sonny Lindner ran the race a total of five times.

Other Quest repeaters who ran the race three times included Gerald Riley, Lorrina Mitchell, Mary Shields, Don Glassburn, and Nick Ericson. Joe Runyan, Jack Hayden, Kevin Turnbough, David Humphrey, Ron Aldrich, Murray Clayton, and Shirley Liss ran the Quest twice. Overall, only 15 percent of mushers run the Yukon Quest four or more times, and 52 percent only make the attempt once.

Eight mushers—2.25 percent—have started the race 10 or more times. Those eight have a combined finished total of 84,000 miles.

The list of those who assisted in the birthing of the Yukon Quest is long. Although it was the dream of two men, it could never have come to fruition without the aid of hundreds of people who shared Shank's and Roger D. Williams's dream and put in thousands of hours to make it come true.

For those who were there at the beginning, it was a time of possibility and excitement—they proved that two men and many volunteers can make a difference and start something new, which has now been around for three decades. On race days, the teams burst from the starting chute, and it's just as exciting now as it was then—just as intoxicating, invigorating, and addicting.

Marti Steury says: "To be a part of putting something like this together was an absolute privilege. I mean, what a privilege to be able to be a part of history that actually recreates history. LeRoy looks at it as though it was his firstborn, and there are a number of us that do as well. To look back and say, 'Wow, the first one is 30 years old,' is remarkable. Some things have changed. Some other things probably never will. This is something that is bigger than the sum of its parts. You have the opportunity to have this be your Quest in whatever way it is for you, and as long as you own this race, it is your race."

Many of those who were there at the beginning eventually drifted away, but there is something about this race. It becomes a part of a person, even if that person never runs it. Sometimes, people leave and come back, including Steury, who wanted to run the race but ended up running the organization instead (she never did get to run the race—her dogs were too old by the time she could). Steury is now the executive director of the Fairbanks Quest organization, a job she reentered in 2009. Like Alaska, this race gets into a person and never really leaves.

The Yukon Quest still attracts diehard fans who volunteer for events, do office work, mark trails, and man checkpoints just to share their love of the sport and the dogs. It attracts people who might never be mushers but just love the sport. The race attracts dog-lovers, mushing fans, and the curious. Some come to see what the race is all about and, satiated, go on with their lives. Others get pulled in to a different world, a world where reality includes feeding and caring for dozens of dogs every day, where weeklong trips in wild and untamed wilderness count as vacations, and where dogs are more than pets—they are partners and colleagues.

Top mushers estimate that it costs about $1,000 per dog per year to run a good kennel. In addition to sponsors, good mushers (i.e., those who win) can sell puppies from their best dogs, often for several thousand dollars. A good lead dog can be worth up to $15,000; as a musher starts winning bigger races and becoming known, pups from his or her kennel become more valuable. Successful mushers are methodical about breeding; they keep detailed records, and dogs are carefully matched to produce the best racing and working animals. Breeders are not afraid to throw in a dog with favorable attributes, even if it is not an Alaskan husky. (Library of Congress.)

DISCOVER THOUSANDS OF LOCAL HISTORY BOOKS FEATURING MILLIONS OF VINTAGE IMAGES

Arcadia Publishing, the leading local history publisher in the United States, is committed to making history accessible and meaningful through publishing books that celebrate and preserve the heritage of America's people and places.

Find more books like this at
www.arcadiapublishing.com

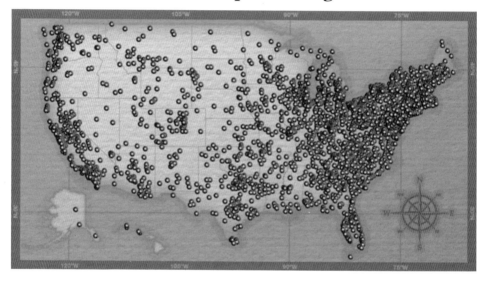

Search for your hometown history, your old stomping grounds, and even your favorite sports team.

Consistent with our mission to preserve history on a local level, this book was printed in South Carolina on American-made paper and manufactured entirely in the United States. Products carrying the accredited Forest Stewardship Council (FSC) label are printed on 100 percent FSC-certified paper.

MADE IN THE USA